"I have learned that if you must leave a place that you have lived in and loved and where all your yesteryears are buried deep, leave it any way except a slow way, leave it the fastest way you can."

—Beryl Markham, *West with the Night*

THE BEJEWELED CHAMELEON

———

LINDA GARZIERA

Copyright 2024 by Linda Garziera

All rights reserved. No part of this publication may be reproduced, distributed, or transmitted in any form of any means, including photocopying, recording, or other electronic or mechanical methods, without the prior written permission of the publisher, except in the case of brief quotations embodied in critical reviews and certain other noncommercial uses permitted by copyright law.

For permission requests, contact Linda Garziera at lindagarziera@gmail.com

Set in EB Garamond.

ISBN: 9798322544319

Cover art by Maggie Largent.
Illustrations, including maps, by Linda Garziera.

Printed by Amazon Kindle Direct Publishing, in the United States of America.

First printing edition 2024.

*For Pino—my best editor,
most careful reader, and my dad.*

And for Panpan, with love.

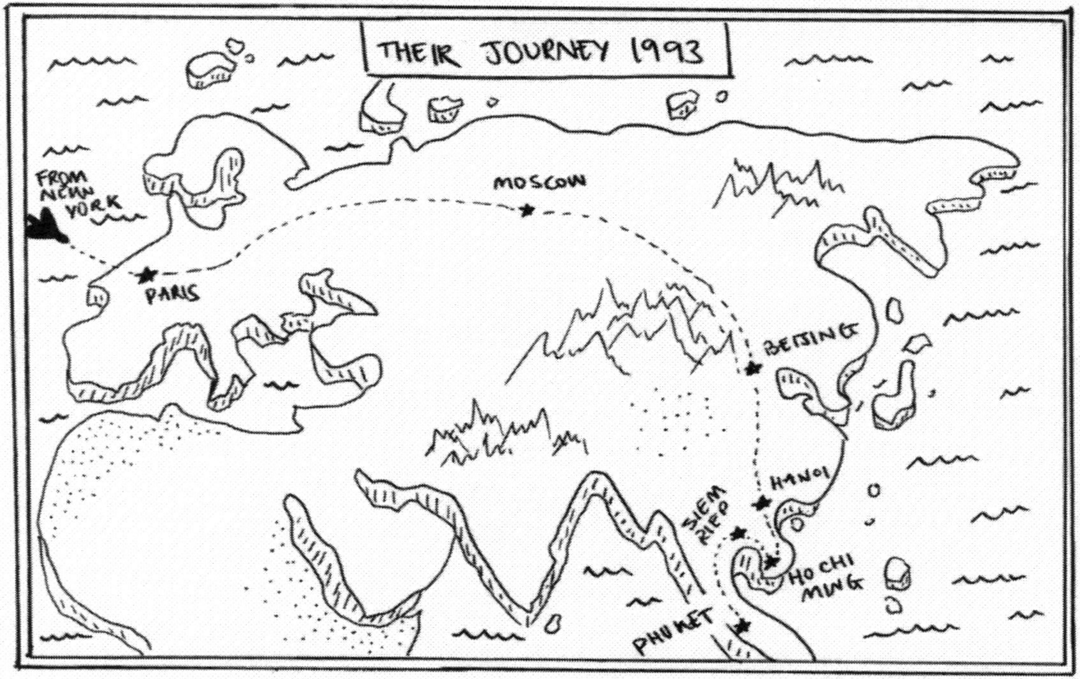
THEIR JOURNEY 1993
FROM NEW YORK
PARIS
MOSCOW
BEIJING
HANOI
SIEM RIEP
HO CHI MING
PHUKET

WANG PHO SUNAN TEMPLE
DARA'S HOUSE
NIGHT MARKET
OLD PHUKET TOWN
BIG MAN'S HOUSE
SEA GYPSY VILLAGE
TAO'S HOUSE
PHUKET CITY

Chapter 1

PHUKET, THAILAND, 1979

THE STEERING WHEEL WAS STICKY with mango juice and hot midday sun. Even with the car bounding down the road, banana trees sweeping forward as the small Nissan made its way towards the exchange point, A-wut couldn't pick up a breeze. His pants were plastered to his thighs, droplets of sweat sat on his nose and lip, which he licked before shifting up a gear and maneuvering the car off the asphalt and onto a dirt path leading to the jungle.

If there wasn't any breeze before—on the open road, a break in the trees—there was even less now. He felt gnats stick to his neck as waves of humidity rolled in. The smell of wet leaves filled the car. Squinting in the semi-dark, he wiped his face with his jacket sleeve and discovered a small viper curled between the empty passenger's seat and the door. He looked at the time. While Thailand was just waking up, he was hurtling into Phuket's forest, checking for snakes in the rearview mirror and airway vents.

Decha was already there when A-wut arrived. He was parked underneath a beautiful Banyan tree, one hundred feet of canopy, branches thick and gorgeous with roots pouring onto the forest floor. It seemed to hang mid-air rather than grow from the earth. With his back to all this, Decha remained leaning on the hood of his own black car even as A-wut killed the engine, grabbed the snake by the neck, flung it into the thicket, and began walking towards him. He was not one to extend a hand in greeting and so offered a grunt instead.

"In there?" A-wut said, peeking in the darkened window.

"Careful, he bites."

"You always say that."

Decha grunted too, pulled a cigar from his breast pocket, and placed it in his mouth without lighting it.

"How much do you think, for this one?" A-wut tried to peek inside again but failed to see much more than a faint silhouette.

"Let's not talk here." Decha glanced about as if the subject was too vulgar for such a place and spat some tobacco on the ground, moving the new Cuban to the other side of his mouth. "It's a good client." He couldn't help but smile some. "If this goes well, we'll eat some shrimp with The Big Man tonight."

They never called The Big Man by his name, and in Thai the nickname seemed to swallow other words. Decha threw the car keys at A-wut and stepped back onto one of the Banyan roots snaking into the undergrowth. His face grew serious.

"You're to be at the airport by seven."

A-wut frowned at the command, but he nodded.

Then, in one motion, he stepped into the car, started the gas, and backed out of the clearing without sparing Decha a second glance. While there were no snakes in this car, a chameleon perching on the dashboard poked his tongue out in what A-wut thought to be an ominous sign. It wasn't until he was back on the banana-lined road headed to the airport that he relaxed enough to look in his rearview mirror.

There, legs pressed against the hard cushion of the seats, hands clutching his knees, was a small boy, five or six. A-wut was almost surprised to find he resembled the previous kid. Save for a white-ish spot underneath his left eye, a stain in the shape of a puddle, the only thing A-wut could pick out were his eyes.

A-wut looked back at the road, cleared his throat a couple of times.

"I've got a daughter. I think she's your age."

It wasn't exactly a question, and the boy didn't reply. He just turned his gaze to the side window, where he could see the highest of Phuket's houses receding in gold and terracotta. Slowly, the Banyan's canopy got smaller and smaller behind the frame of the car.

Chapter 2

IT WAS ONLY ELEVEN AND the two men had already reduced three packs of cigarettes to stubs and flicked them out their car window. The night was pouring rain, coming down in heavy drops that ran down the windshield like snail trails. Nothing in New York is ever handed to you gently. Yet, on this particular day, the two men felt like the sky was taking aim and hawking it all up—vomit reek in the alleyways, piss on Wall Street, and all the Central Park dog shit—onto their roof.

They kept their windows down though, deciding to smoke and suffer the wet. The men talked the way sailors talk: passing a travel-sized whiskey bottle, cupping the lighter for one another, growling at the rain. It was a miserable day on the west side of JFK airport—trash spilling out of waterlogged dumpsters, rats lurking under grates, jets rumbling unseen above the clouds—the rain and the smoke in the car just made it more so.

"What time are they supposed to get here?"
"One."

"Hmm."

"Yup."

They were parked in shadow from the front of the airport, where they could still see people exit without themselves being seen. A young family was arguing with a taxi driver just ahead, close enough for them to see the man's wet glasses and the white smoke coming in puffs from the driver's open window. Further on, an airport traffic controller in orange high-viz was hunched against the rain while he directed cars away from the clogged pick up line.

"These airlines," the man at the wheel started, before stopping to watch the father of the family resign to a corner of the airport tent.

"What?"

"Does it always rain so much in New York?"

"So they say."

"Yes I know—" He cut himself off and spent a long time scratching his sideburns. After a while, he seemed to forget he had said anything at all.

"I think you're still getting used to it." In the passenger seat, the man sported an orange and blue Knicks hat, its rigid brim sticking out like a beak, hair poking out through the mesh sides. He tilted the hat at a group of people running from the airport to a cab on the opposite side of the street.

"D'you know that you can tell if someone is a tourist by how well they respond to the weather? Take those people. Anyone who's spent some time in the city in the summer, when it storms this bad, would know that holding any amount of stuff to your head does absolutely nothing for the rain. And anyone who's ever been here more than once knows that if you walk under that ledge, through the parking garage, there are about a dozen free cabs waiting on the other side."

He shook his head as the cab he'd been observing drove off. The bearded man didn't give any hint that he'd been listening, ducking to check the arrivals board again, frowning. They passed cigarettes back and forth as more planes grumbled overhead. Time dragged. They lit new cigarettes and drained the whiskey.

"Tourists and locals, right," said the bearded man eventually, as if he'd been mulling the statement over in his head and had just come up with a response, "and which of the two wears a dumb hat like yours?"

Really, the hat man didn't care about the game or the team all that much. They were playing in a state he hadn't bothered to remember and the hat, which seemed to have been molded around a soccer ball, now dug into his forehead. But its color had brought up an argument about its *conspicuousness* earlier and he couldn't give his companion the satisfaction by taking it off. So he merely sighed, watching some water droplets fall from the visor to his lap. It poured and it poured and the Knicks were playing somewhere.

"What do you say I grab another bottle?" the bearded man said finally, giving his face a break and picking up the empty one. He was fond of New York because, regardless of which direction you might walk in, you will find a convenience store every two blocks. He looked at the blinking green lights on the opposite street corner. *Open! Open!* He was especially fond of seven-elevens and their impossible hours—where else could a man get an honest bottle of booze at two in the morning?

As he opened the car door, however, he slipped on a wet manhole cover, and in the flailing of hands, sent the glass bottle flying into the pavement.

"Ngì ngèā. The whole point we're in this dank corner is to hide," the man in the car spat out as the taxi driver in front of them leaned out his window toward the noise. Even the father of the soaked family looked up from his misery.

The sideburns man had fallen butt first into a puddle. He said nothing as he peeled a slimy candy wrapper from his thigh and dragged his water-heavy shoes onto the pavement, trudging off toward the Seven Eleven. Truth is, he hadn't noticed the noise at all.

The hat man checked his watch when he noticed sideburns man sloshing his way back to the car through the flooded curbside. It was now one in the morning. The father of the family was moving suitcases away from a homeless man squatting underneath the sagging tent with raw hot dogs and a pot to catch the water. All the onlookers wondered how he planned to light a fire. Sideburns man had taken his time inside the Seven Eleven and, instead of whiskey, was carrying six boxes of Anthon Berg liquor chocolates, red and blue and stamped with tiny labels of famous brands, each pretty and nostalgic like toy wax figurines. Climbing back into the car, his sideburns seemed redder than ever.

"They don't sell whiskey."

Soaked like a cat after a bath and dripping on the boxes as he set them in his lap, he gave a tentative smile.

"They're Memorial Day themed."

They began working through the first set, biting off the chocolate caps, swallowing the teaspoon of liquor inside, and then nibbling on the rest. In the meantime, the Arrivals board remained frozen.

"Do we wait for them to come out or do we go in?"

"I say we wait."

"You think they'll look odd?"

"What, a man, a woman and a kid? They should look like a family. Unless they're acting funny."

The hat man swallowed a cap whole and made a face. "Phracêā chwy. Acting funny? They better not. We warned them. We—"

"I know, I know. They're late, that's all."

They each drained the alcohol in their bottles and ate in silence.

The sideburns man glanced toward the airport and then back at the bottles. He lowered his voice. "They just have to act natural."

"But what if they *inspect* their documents?"

The sideburns man ignored him. "Ngī̀ ngèā, the plane is late." He looked up at the black sky and huffed. Just then, the soaked family must have convinced the taxi for a ride, because they disappeared in the car and the driver laid on his horn as he tried moving through the traffic. He waited for the hollering to fade into the distance before continuing. "How is it they got flights coming in this late on Memorial Day?"

The other man sighed, carefully cracking each of his knuckles. "It's the weather."

"That's not fair." He was always saying how things weren't fair, scratching his sideburns and pinching his beard between his thumb and forefinger, something he often did when miserable situations got even more miserable still. "Not fair at all."

At that same moment, in a small office in the back hallways of the airport, high above their dented Kia sedan, a team of middle-aged men with shiny nametags and shinier foreheads congratulated each other over winning the war. Holding small flags, they threw around jokes about the Redcoats and risqué comments about their wives, chuckling and acting like the inch of champagne in their glass was quite enough to get them drunk. On this particular day, the party spirit was really rolling all over America.

"Hey," the man stopped tapping on the wheel to point across the parking lot, "is that cop coming toward us?"

Through the pouring sheets of rain, they watched a policeman waiting on the other side of the road for the traffic to ease.

"Yeah," hat man said, poking his head out of the window to see better and wiping the rain from his eyes, "he is."

"Maybe he's just doing his walk around."

"I think he's looking at us."

"No, he isn't," bearded man said, before squinting through the rain. "You think?"

The officer raised a hand, stopping traffic as he stepped off the curb, and began to stride across the pavement.

"Ngỉ ngèā. Is this even legal?" hat man said, gesturing to the boxes in their laps.

The other man touched his beard, caught off guard. "I don't know."

Meanwhile, now on their side of the road, the cop was walking in their direction, ducking against some columns of water trickling down from the lampposts.

"Quick!"

The two men were halfway through the first box of liquor chocolates when they first noticed the cop. Now, they began gulfing down the bottles two and three at a time, the bearded man finishing the last row while hat man shoved the rest of the boxes beneath his feet and wiped his fingers on his pants. They managed to fold the empty carton and throw it in the back just as the officer lowered his head and peered through the open window.

The rain drummed on the car roof, so he talked loudly into their car. "Is everything all right here?"

The bearded man was quite obviously forcing a clump of chocolate down his throat. So, even though his own teeth were still covered in chocolate, the hat man replied.

"Yup. All good here, officer." he swallowed some sweet residue and shuddered. The rain seemed to make his ears ring, or maybe it was the liquor at last. Nodding toward the police officer's nametag—*Clinton*, it read, followed by some numbers—he added, "That's like the president, no?"

"Excuse me?"

"Clint-Clinton."

The officer stared at him for a second before nodding towards the bearded man who had managed to swallow at last and was panting from the effort.

"Is he alright?"

"Yes, he's just eating a snack, officer."

For a few seconds, Officer Clinton watched the two clean some of the brown from their teeth. "You waiting for someone?"

The men shared a quick glance. Despite the rain, the car suddenly seemed too quiet. Sideburns stole a glance at the

Arrivals board before returning his attention to Officer Clinton.

"The flight is late." His voice was squeaky, not entirely from the sugar coating his throat.

Officer Clinton frowned but he shook his head. "Little bit ago I saw you throw a glass bottle just outside on the curb?"

The bearded man let out a breath. "That was an accident, I slipped in the water and—" he looked at his companion and then back at the officer, "I swear, it was an accident."

Officer Clinton wiped off some rain that had collected on his eyebrows. He started to say something and then thought better of it. The rain became even heavier on his slumped shoulders.

"It's Memorial Day, Clint."

The two men waited, the taste in their mouth bitter from the chocolates. The homeless man coughed underneath the tent.

"Alright, I'll just give you a warning. I'll get your license plate number." But he just stepped back from the car, pulled out a pack of gum and put one in his mouth. "You might want to roll up your windows."

For the first time in an hour, the Arrivals board showed that several new flights had landed. The men scanned them and swore under their breath.

"Yes, yes, happy twenty-seventh Clint." The bearded man said, wiping his wet fringe from his forehead.

The hat man was still staring at the board. "Those can't be the last planes to land today. They can't."

"What?" Officer Clinton looked up into the sky, shaking droplets from his head, and stepped closer to the car.

"It was a one A.M. arrival," hat man said under his breath. He kicked a box at his feet, dropping the hat on it. He fumbled with his last cigarette and lit it. "No worries Clint, thanks again."

And with that they rolled up their windows and moved the car about a block, parking it in another dark and rainy corner of the airport, leaving Officer Clinton to run through traffic and the misery of the night. It seemed that the only person having a fine time on Memorial Day that year was the homeless man eating raw hot dogs at two in the morning.

The bearded man took up another cigarette himself. A little damp, it reminded him of the cheap fireworks he used to buy at a Dxkmîpheling stand as a child. He struggled to light it.

"It was one a.m. One o'clock at terminal C, goddammit. We're at terminal C."

He spat out of the window and held the cigarette away from the rain, revealing a punctured tattoo on his right forearm. A H̥awh̄ñā kǽng, a gang leader, had drawn it outside his elementary school in Phuket—it was a snake eating another snake eating another snake again and again in a smudgy little circle. Really, it looked like a badly sketched smiley face, but people would assume it was a burn mark and so, naturally, that he was part of a gang. And that, besides dealing with actual gangs, had always served him well.

"We're at terminal C, right?"

It was now the other's turn to ignore the question. The hat man wiped his fingers on the damp layers of his coat, opened the glove compartment and extracted a limp napkin that had the flight's information written on the back. He took a long time reading it.

"We are at C *right*? We aren't—"

"One o'clock, Terminal C, *Newark Airport*," hat man said dryly.

The bearded man didn't reply immediately. "What did you say?"

"It says one o'clock and Terminal C. But this is JFK you fool, you got the wrong airport. Can't you read? *Did* you read this before we left?" His voice trembled, as if the rain had gotten to him at last. He ground his fingers into his temples.

For a moment they held their breath, reading the napkin over again. Then, they fired up the engine, threw their stubs into the gutter, put up the windows and peeled away toward Newark.

At the right airport, a young boy was standing ever so still in front of a candy store, his fists clenched around the straps of his backpack. He was fixed in front of the cotton candy machine, which was spinning blue in a beautiful cloud for a little girl. A man and a woman stood close; the boy felt the woman's knees bump against him. They couldn't talk in English and so they didn't talk at all. In Thailand, the rain season was just beginning.

Chapter 3

LIKE EVERY YEAR, UPTOWN BUILDINGS still adorned with Christmas decorations, brown snow frozen along the curbs, and Fifth Avenue doormen savoring the arrival of grand clients and even grander tips to come with the festivities, preparations for the Chinese New Year began. For most New Yorkers, those preparations would appear to start much later, around mid-January, when groups of children first scattered through the city to help plaster red and gold posters on subway cars and in public bathrooms, announcing the date and the new year's zodiac animal. They would arrive with the sudden intensity of red crocuses lining Central Park in spring.

But if one were to sit in a tea house in the early days of December, even one on the less visited outskirts of Chinatown, and really look at the city, they would find the arrangements well under way: old ladies dusting carpets on their balconies, their granddaughters returning home with cases of oranges and candles; small groups of men with ladders and carrying baskets of lanterns bigger than themselves, setting up at every street corner to string up the decorations. That same viewer would see splashes of color and statues popping up in window sills and bus stops, the subtle, early signs of the coming transformation.

Felix observed these changes from the entrance of a steamy dumpling shop which bordered the old Jewish neighborhood on Hester street. It was a cramped space, all metal chairs and knees, ads in Cantonese and condensation blurring the windows, so he had decided to wait for Selena outside. It was a pleasantly cold night, as it had been for the past few New Years, and he was giddy from the brightening new year's landscape and the prospect of turning nineteen. With the city gearing up for the biggest celebrations of the year, his birthday had arrived.

But his birthday had never been a big deal.

Growing up, his parents would stack doughnuts on a paper plate instead of getting him a cake, and he'd stay up all night playing video games with his brother Zion. But it wasn't a *special day* in the way a mall sales clerk would wish you to have, placing a hand on your arm, maybe handing you a soap sample. It was a day like any other.

Felix's adoptive parents, Nelson and Selena, were not gift-giving types. They celebrated his birthdays the quiet way, cooking elaborate dinners and watching Felix's favorite movie with the sunset dipping into their cocoa mugs. Because of that, the only real gift he ever received was from Aunt Mertha, following her death, when—the funeral over and their lives resumed—her ashes arrived.

The urn itself was a poorly executed piece that was supposed to resemble the head of an Akhal-Teke horse, looking—instead of a proud steed from Turkmenistan—like a scrawny, disproportionate thing. Its neck, instead of long and elegant like that of the real horse, recalled a fallen tree stump, and as such, proved great for picking socks off the floor. Felix's brother Zion had named it Hercules, after its professed grandeur.

The vase was made from Murano glass, milky and more expensive than anything else in the Laudrey house. Half-transparent and light, the boys would shake it like a snowglobe and watch the ashes pour down from the horse's eyes. They called it the Mertha Hourglass. When he started smoking, Zion would tap his cigarettes into a crack near Hercules's left ear, a wound from a particularly rough game. So, slowly, unnoticed, Aunt Mertha's presence grew.

That is what Selena would have said, anyway. A converted Buddhist, she believed in karma and the continuation of the spirit after death. To Felix, it seemed that by keeping her sister's ashes in her house, Selena was condemning the woman to haunt their house for good. While he was used to being confused by almost anything Aunt Mertha had ever done, Felix didn't understand this wish from his mother.

All he really remembered about his aunt was his seventh birthday when he'd been locked in a chokehold under her armpits, listening to her spit about politics even after their mother left the room. Her vaseline and foxhound smell had lingered on the furniture for days. The memory remained vivid.

The day itself had been cold and rainy, that boring time of February when Chinatown celebrations were over and Aunt

Mertha came to visit. Seven year old Felix had just woken up and was heading to the living room for breakfast, when she sprung from behind the fridge door and asked him for a chat. *Sprung* was perhaps not the right word for her movement. It was more of a heave, a labored waddle that ended with a grunt.

"So, you're already seven. It's exciting, yeah? You're having fun, yeah? What's that? Now let's not get carried away, it's just a birthday after all. What's that? No, let's talk for a while, let's make tea. *Mhmm. Mhmm.* Make it a ginger one, sweet lamb, with sugar."

Felix still remembered the cold feeling of the water as it ran down his fingers while his aunt peppered him with questions and inane comments. When he checked the time, it had only been two minutes.

"How do you and Zion get along?"

"He's not half bad when he wants to be."

He watched Aunt Mertha's left eye start to droop. She had some medical condition that made her look appalled all the time, especially to hear Felix challenge Zion's integrity like that. In all honesty, Zion would have probably agreed with him. He never had much integrity for being a Boy Scout.

"Mhmm." This sound she would make often—scraping the back of her throat for something to say. "Mhmm," she repeated, "I've always thought that you had one of the faces where you can just...tell."

The whistle of the teapot saved Felix from replying. She evidently thought she was being clever—on what, Felix wasn't too sure—but he was busy concentrating on her eye, the lid fluttering grossly and the pupil inching closer to the bottom. He turned away.

"Yes Aunt Mertha." If he squinted hard enough, their rose teapot looked like an old man.

"Back at Zion's age I don't know if I would've played with you either. You know how it is."

He knew perfectly how it was. If she'd been his age, he wouldn't have had anything to do with her. She would have been hanging toes-up on the monkey bars and probably even then calling him a sweet lamb or pork chop or some abomination of an animal. It served her right, he'd consider later, for her ashes to be cast into the hideous form of Hercules.

"Did you get a haircut?"

"No."

"I thought so. You should, *mhmm?*"

She raked a hand through her dyed hair in a way that exposed her red-stained skull and all the grease. He tried not to make a face. His mother's curls were messy and loud and a warm gold like the doughnuts he knew were waiting for him in the living room. He found his mother beautiful. Conversely, Aunt Mertha looked as distasteful as she acted.

Felix remembered that he had been counting the tiles on the kitchen ceiling, waiting for her to let him go, when, glancing at her, he noticed that her pupil disappeared completely. Felix stopped short, not knowing what to say as she looked at him through one eye. Aunt Mertha, however, didn't seem to notice this change, instead she narrowed her other eye and continued without pause.

"Make me another cup, mhmm? What a dear, what a dear." She stopped to scratch a mole above her lip with her thumb. "Felix, say, what do you see when you look in the mirror?"

Even at seven, Felix figured he would never fully understand the woman, but even so, he could sense her working up a dirty trick.

He answered tentatively. "Myself?"

"No, sweetie. Well, what do you see when you look at Zion?" She said, probing. But Felix remained quiet until she continued. She clicked her tongue.

"Nothing to be done about you, mhmm? Maybe you wouldn't even understand. But, I do think you're old enough. Have you not figured it out already? Mhmm? I mean just look at yourself—"

And it was in the kitchen, a hot cup of ginger tea in his hands, that the big whale of a woman who smelled of sticky face cream and dog and who yammered on unceasingly told him for the second time that he was adopted.

"Doesn't it all make more sense now darling?" She exclaimed, her other eye beginning to roll back. "Now run along like a good little kid. And—oh, you absolute dear, bless you. You didn't even spill the tea."

Within the Laudrey house, bare of curtains and door keys, Nelson and Selena lived without secrets. They had never pretended that Felix wasn't adopted, and it had never bothered him. Presumably, he would have realized it himself even if he hadn't been told. Selena, thick-boned and tall, had frizzy hair that caught the sun like a cloud of bees, all gold and tanned skin. Nelson sported freckles and a Roman nose, white hair that was once ginger, always bemused by something. Zion was like neither really, but he had an appearance that could only be borne from a Laudrey. Felix, as Aunt Mertha was trying to point out, was Asian.

―――――――

It had been a very brisk night the day Selena and Nelson first met Felix. They had been on a spiritual retreat with fellow bohemians on a base of the Himalayas in Nepal, where they had dabbled in Hinduism and spicy curries and the discomfort of foregoing a shower. It had been life changing: after sleeping together in a hammock, the flight back—stocked with purified water, a flushing toilet and padded seating—had been the best fifteen sleeping hours of their lives.

As they got off the flight, they were completely Zen. Waiting for their taxi in the lobby, they didn't immediately notice a small child, perhaps five years old, sitting on his knees by the bathroom, reducing a luggage label to bits. Had the waiting room been full he would have been swallowed by the noise, but there were only a few people besides them. They smiled when they took his hand and asked for his name. They were Zen when he didn't understand them.

They decided they would take him home and bring him to a foster home the next day, and they continued talking about the yaks and the mountains they had seen as they climbed in a cab and directed the driver. The child was sitting in between them, nibbling on his backpack strap. Underneath his drying tears was a stain in the shape of a puddle. Just under a month later they adopted him.

―――――――

Felix had moved to sit on a bench in front of the shop, and was now watching a man wheel boxes of sprouts into a restaurant across the street. He noticed a paper rooster stuck on the man's jacket and chuckled. With his actual birthdays being days with no presents and too often taken over by memories of Aunt Mertha and of the airport, he preferred celebrating Chinese New Year.

In the lead-up to new year's day, he would explore all kinds of markets, eating squid rings on sticks while venturing in and out of conversation with butchers and calligraphy artists and out-of-season mooncake bakers. Each year he was taken by something new: oriental dances he'd watch with Selena, dragon parades he attended with his dad and brother, leaving early for a big lunch in the heart of *Chinaland*, as Zion used to call it, of *Chun Juan* and fish. It really was his favorite time of year— Christmas trees still peeking from curtains, confetti shrapnel on the Empire State steps, the bustling activity of Asian markets storing up for the big event.

It was also the only time of year he could speak Thai. Alongside the flowering of New York's Chinese community came Thai puppeteers, Khon mask painters, *pad thai* tossed in large woks. He would navigate streets filled by Indonesian batik sellers, large pots of Singaporean fried rice, Japanese mochi craftsmen, pounding and pounding the colorful dough into neat little globes.

Although there was always more than he could see at the festival, he had always wanted to travel to Thailand himself. Among the few possessions he had in his backpack when they found him at the airport was a small journal with an address, *Chalong, Mueang Phuket District, Phuket*. Before adopting him, Selena and Nelson had sent a letter to the address with stamp money, but a reply never came.

How he had come to America was something they couldn't answer, so Felix came to assume that he had been sent by his family for a better life. But, besides a certain wondering about his childhood, he didn't think about it much. Only occasionally, when a Taa Yai rolled her sweet pork buns from a quiet kitchen onto a kiosk and sat drinking cardamom tea as the buns' aroma wafted about the market, he would find himself brought back to the memory of his first house. He remembered little of Thailand—hot cabbage soup, heavy rain on the terracotta porch, straw cabinets filled with ceramic bowls—but he knew he wanted to go back. Which is why he spent the months before New Year inside Chinatown, picking up odd jobs to save up.

There was one man on Canal Street he would work for every year. Mr Wanchai owned a sizable seafood restaurant that would be packed from the morning of Chinese New Year to the next. So, starting three days before the actual day, Felix would help Mr Wanchai unload the delivery truck into the tiny kitchen at the back. Because fish is thought to bring good luck for the new year, Mr Wanchai had some three tons of fresh mud carp and catfish specially sourced for the big day. He was not the type of man that shied away from abundance.

While he was also a generous man—cooking Felix two meals and three for himself—he refused to hire more than one chef to prep the massive amount of fish. The job was tedious and repetitive; Mr Wanchai was particular about how Felix cut into the fish, and the fish themselves were particular to being held—some slipped away, some gave to the knife, while some seemed to have bones everywhere. Felix's hands would smell for days. The kitchen would be layered in slime, fins and viscera Mr Wanchai had Felix cut off, shouting the orders in Chinese until Felix caught on. The work was so gross, and Mr Wanchai so irritable, that Felix *had* to return each year—how could he not? After all, he believed that no one, among the thousands that ate in Mr Wanchai's restaurant the subsequent nights, would have otherwise helped him.

Nelson and Selena were holding hands when they walked in with Felix. The three of them piled into the dumpling house and ordered without a menu. They sipped on green tea while they waited for their food and kept watch for open seats. Felix was accustomed to the movements of such places and knew that three chairs could clear quickly and be taken just as fast, so they each scattered around the room. Soon, their patience was rewarded: just as their number was called, a whole group of people left a table, and they were the first to claim it.

As he placed his own bowl of *jiaozi* and broth in front of an empty seat and helped Selena with the array of other dishes they had ordered, he couldn't help but grin at the chaos: the air warm and a little sticky, people talking over one another, bowls passed, broth spilled, the stillness of the street outside. They would come here every year around his birthday. The ritual was a private celebration, nodding toward new zodiac decorations, listening to the loud hubbub of Cantonese and chopsticks.

"Oh my God." Selena would always attack the fried dumplings first, dipping them in soy sauce and eating them whole. "So good."

Felix took a bite of a pillowy pork bun while his own dumplings cooled.

"Nineteen." Nelson said, weighing the word in a deliberate manner, so that it dawned on them all over again. "You've grown up Lixie."

"Yup," he looked outside as a group of children passed, packing snowballs, red envelopes sticking out of their back pockets, "I can't believe a year has passed already."

That was a lie. He had taken a gap year from school to work and had kept his hands busy with fish guts at Mr Wanchai's place and odd repair jobs, bouncing like a pinball between the boroughs. On the subway, a toolbox in his lap, he had many times felt that the year was passing with incredible slowness, everything building up and digging into his knees.

Truth is, he was nervous at the idea of being nineteen, but he also felt giddy: working so much, he had finally made enough for a ticket.

"Baby?" Selena looked at him and frowned. As usual, she was all soft shapes and colors, wearing a long satin skirt that hung against her thighs and contrasted with the otherwise industrial feel of the restaurant. Nelson was twisting jade prayer beads around his wrist. Felix couldn't help chuckle.

"Listen," he took a couple breaths, "you know I never really want anything for my birthday."

"Right, well," Nelson had finished his food already and was watching Felix play with his, "You can, if you want."

"I know, I didn't mean it like that." The shop was full of loud talking and feet shuffling. The little hiccups in his speech.

"No, I like our celebration. Just, I've made a good bit of money this year," he looked up from his jiaozi, his knees were bouncing, "I was thinking of finally going to Thailand. I'm going to send a fax to that number again. Just in case." his throat closed momentarily but he cracked a smile.

His parents reacted in the only way they could, ordering a feast fit for the Terracotta Army and their descendants. Selena had started singing *One Night in Bangkok* but changed the lyrics, *Phuket*.

Nelson cupped a hand on Felix's shoulder as plates upon plates piled on their table. "You're still up for the dragon parade next week, or is it even worth it?"

Felix just smiled, knowing they would go and they would sing along to all the songs and light fireworks that night. Chinese New Year was just around the corner, the western year still fresh and blazing, oranges bloomed in Guǒyuán gardens all around Chinatown, and it was finally his birthday.

He picked up a fresh bowl of broth and blew.

Chapter 4

IN THE FOURTEEN YEARS HE'D lived in New York, Felix had learned his own way around the city. He had grown from a curious, restless child into the same kind of young man. The streets of his neighborhood, and the alleyways with cheap soda dispensers that lay on its perimeter, knew him just as well as he knew them, each year having pushed the boundaries his parents set. Nelson and Selena warned him of all the usual things—strangers, the dark, and they had a knack for making an impression. Thus Felix had kept to himself, and gradually, by growing older alongside the cracks of the city, he built a reputation as a kid to be reckoned with.

Zion didn't buy into his parents' spiritual daze, and he also spent more time on the streets than off them. He was a bit more cowboy, outdoorsy with calloused hands, making camp in skate parks and catching the very last subway ride home. Tucked in his belt loop was an old screw tin filled with mints, which he would offer to everyone except Felix. On hearing the news about Thailand, he slapped his brother's neck with a heavy hand and raised his glass.

"And if you see a pretty lady—" He winked and drained the milk in one large gulp.

They were brothers at home and rivals on the street. Besides that, they kept to themselves and their lonesome wandering. When Felix thought about it, there was really no one he could imagine going to Thailand with. Save of course for Boon.

Felix found him where he thought he would. It was two weeks after dumpling night, and the weight of nineteen was sitting comfortably like a pin on his chest as he jogged across the street, entering Danny's bar on Seventh and inhaling the smoke.

The bar was busy sorting out lunchtime, but he spotted Boon easily enough through the crowd. It was a new, hipster place, with seriously dim lights, too much flannel and too many non-alcoholic beer drinkers for a good hangout. Felix raised his eyebrows as he moved past bearded men running their fingers on the rims of their fedoras the way girls might worry over their diamond earrings at a ball.

He spotted Boon right away, one of the few clean-cut heads in the place, sporting his usual mint suit with pants worn at the knees—something eccentric and unusual even for a man in marketing. He was on the phone, smiling and taking sips of his beer. He ended the call just as Felix settled into the stool next to him and ordered an orange juice for himself, not trusting the colorful non-alcoholic beverages on the menu.

"Same tab, thanks," he said to the bartender.

"Really? The same tab?" Boon said. However, he nodded at the bartender then passed the drink to Felix, but not before taking a sip himself.

"You had to?" Felix also drank, then wiped his mouth on his jacket sleeve. Boon didn't seem to hear him. "You seem happy."

Boon frowned a little, but then he smiled again. "I am."

"Who were you talking to?"

"My wife."

Felix raised his eyebrows. Boon hadn't been in a serious relationship in four years, and, Felix knew, he was just too pleased with himself about it.

Still, picking up the sarcasm, Feilx said, "Married? Congratulations, though it's not very *hipster* of you. How've you been otherwise?"

"You know, work, home to the wife, driven out to *cool* bars…"

"No kidding."

Boon grinned but turned his head. He didn't in fact have a wife, but he felt that it was quite hipster to have one at home and complain about it at a bar.

"How's work?" Felix continued.

"Awful."

"Really?"

"Slow."

"Good."

They fell silent for a moment, their attention shifting momentarily to a group in black tanks comparing bicep tattoos in the far corner. Boon sipped his beer thoughtfully before handing it to Felix who also took a sip. His mouth twitched. It was pretty awful beer.

"I just—" Boon said suddenly.

"Want to quit? I know." Felix replied, as he did every time the subject came up.

"It could work, you know."

"What, selling whiskey?"

"Yeah. It's—" Boon shook his head. He wasn't attached to advertising. At first he'd been fascinated with its rhythms, working late into the night to make deadlines, drinking on the job to ease the pressure. But both would be true were he selling whiskey. There was a small distillery on Raquette Lake in the upstate for sale that he had seen in the newspaper that morning. Still, he was in a funny mood and didn't want to discuss it. "Nothing."

"You know," Felix said, "each time you pitch me the plan I almost think you might actually be adequate at marketing."

"Thanks."

"But you need money to buy a distillery." Felix observed.

"I know."

"And training."

Boon made a face. "*Thanks* for the wisdom."

"Yeah, no problem. The advice is free."

Boon ordered another juice for Felix and took a large gulp before passing it on.

Felix shifted in his seat. "You *had* to?"

"I *am* paying for this." But he raised his glass to Felix's.

"C'mon this is a bore."

"In a hurry?" said Boon.

"You're right. We should stay here cause this is such a great spot."

Boon chuckled. He gave Felix a good look over and involuntarily his grin softened. "Okay, lets get outta here. This beer sucks."

"What, your keto, gluten-free, sugar-free hipster concoction that smells like pears instead of beer isn't working?"

"Why'd you come here? Just to bust my chops?" Boon demanded.

"Well, I wanted to change up the crowd. The bad beer is a plus."

"Gimme a break." He had been in a state all day, but there was something curious about Felix too. Boon's eyes narrowed. "Really, what brought you here?"

"A fan."

"A *fan?*"

"Jesus, I forgot you were so paranoid."

Just then the bar got very loud as one of the pool players scored a point or game and his bearded hipster friends rushed to the counter to order another round of beers or what was sold under that name. The two waited for everyone to get their drinks and return to the back of the room.

"Really, how free are you at work?"

"Quite. I did all my quotas, got a big deal with the perfume witch last week. They'll leave me alone for a while."

"Good," Felix said, glancing evasively at the pool players, feeling Boon's eyes all over the back of his head. "Well," he said, turning around again, unable to hide his smile. "Because I'm going to buy some plane tickets."

Boon barked a laugh, tugging at his ever more loosened tie. He shook his head, "Alright. Is there anything else—"

"*And* one of the tickets is for you." It was Felix's turn to laugh now, but he told him about the trip in a rush. When he was finished he started humming *One Night in Bangkok* under his breath. He picked up the empty glass of juice, went to drink from it, but set it down clumsily on the counter behind him.

Boon had a curious expression. His hand reached into his pocket for his company cell phone but he simply held it. He ordered another round of orange juice, this time for himself.

"What is it?" Felix asked.

"Nothing. It's just a coincidence. I've been wanting to go to Thailand myself." he said, draining the last of the juice in one gulp. Then he winked and Felix grinned back. Both knew he would go, but Felix needed him to say it. Whatever Felix had seen in his expression, gone.

"So you're coming?"

Boon shrugged. "You think they've won or something?' he replied, pointing at the pool players, but he was beaming.

In most bars, the late hours would first see burly men arrive in shirtsleeves despite the cold, itching for the burn of liquor with the readiness of bills and grins akin only to those familiar with the trade. The women with thin collar bones and thick ankles would then enter in a flurry of red lips and murmured compliments. Those in old love followed, holding the doors open, wiping a wet layer of snow from each other's coats, a touch to the jaw. And later, with the moon all big and romantic, young men would stop in for a drink and observe the opulence of the city through the people living in it, and they might even twirl their fingers round the rims of their glasses like girls in love with the night again.

In the hipster bar, everything odd and unusual, the clientele remained the same merry people who had been there since Felix had arrived. There was something stagnant about the neon lights and noncommittal jukebox tune. But as he watched Boon jump up from his stool, swig the last bit of beer from his glass and pay his check with a fat fifty, he felt on top of the world.

Chapter 5

THE NINETEENTH ARRONDISSEMENT IN PARIS—like Central Station in Milan or Washington Park in Chicago—is a quarter you enter only to get your wallet stolen, a black eye, or both. Tucked away in its alleys are smokey pool bars, *Tabac* shops with taped up windows, men huddled on the metro stairs glaring at every passer-by. It is a place for the quick handed and smooth spoken, where you have to know the cobblestones lest they deceive you.

And so, naturally, it was amidst this romantic architecture and its shadows where A-wut was waiting for Decha.

He was leaning against an unsteady railing overlooking the Saint-Denis canal as he studied the street. He took in men opening rusty verandas, flames licking *crêpe* pans at vagabond kiosks, stray cats prowling the street for river rats. When he got bored, he turned to stare at the canal's dense, brown water and ducks caught amid the oil slicks.

He spat on a buoy.

It was seven in the morning, but it felt as if the day was already tired of itself and reaching for dusk. A-wut folded his sunglasses back into his pocket and squinted through the graying park on the other side of the canal. In late spring, when leaves would break free and the river would be a shade or two lighter, the park might almost be picturesque. But that, A-wut thought, lighting a cigarette, was not something he particularly cared to see.

He had been waiting for several hours already—Decha never announced his arrival, so A-wut had to sit out the whole day for their meetings. He often thought about leaving a note and phone number in the agreed spot while he ran other errands. More often than not, he dismissed the thought before it took hold. Still, he carried a pen and notepad with him just in case he might one day find the nerve to do it.

As the hours crawled by and people met and left each other on the street, A-wut kept watch over the various goings-on in the park, blowing into his hands when they grew cold. After some time the ducks began putting on a show for him, flurries of feathers and water spray. A lot of squawking. Later, a man approached him, asked for directions that A-wut couldn't help with, and walked on. Then the waiting continued as before.

A-wut thought back to the case. The Big Man had a liking for drama and had called a large meeting with the group, but ultimately they had all agreed about the threat. This Felix kid had a good disguise—posing as the Big Man's son—and that meant he had something up his sleeve. Whether it was money or something else he wanted, A-wut and Decha had been told to intercept him and follow.

Absentmindedly, A-wut scratched his shoulder where a large Thai flower was tattooed, conspicuous more than necessary and something the Big Man had designed with lavishness in mind.

For an organization which worked in the shadows and dealt with such a delicate trade, A-wut thought the Big Man lacked discretion. In fact, if he and a few others hadn't urged caution at the meeting, the Big Man would've taken direct action. Instead, having talked him into investigating first, A-wut was idling in this godawful park, waiting for Decha to arrive with more information from their lead in New York. If only he had the decency to be on time—

Like the shadows cast along the pavement, A-wut forced himself to move slowly, smoking cigarette after cigarette as he tried to calm himself. That is, until he finally spotted Decha. He coughed as he took a breath.

In all the years he'd known Decha, he still didn't know his full name. Part of it was to hide their identities—yet again, neither were the warmest of men. Decha was a six foot two giant with sinewy arms and legs, a neck like a bull, and a voice that could challenge the Golden Gate foghorns. Outside of Thailand's forests, his expression grew meaner, or more pronounced by the lack of things to distract from it. A thick cigar smell always clung about him. He too took his time walking over to the little notch on grass that A-wut had claimed, smiling at a nearby group of gloved children clamoring around a tent for birthday cake. It was a nice spot, where a stone walkway started towards the water. Once more, A-wut spat out the bad taste in his mouth.

"He's here." Decha said.

A-wut remained silent. They hadn't worked together in years and neither was excited to start again, because in their world, having the Big Man breathing down their necks was never a good sign. Together now, they listened to the children's shrieks as they fought over a mess of frosting and fruit, singing a birthday song in french. Decha began flicking a gold lighter on and off with his sleeve. A-wut tried to spit again but his mouth was dry.

"What did our boys say in New York?" Decha asked, speaking in Thai.

"That he's headed to Phuket, passing through Paris first. Something about an Aunt."

Decha nodded. "Not his."

It was evident that he already knew everything and was just testing how much A-wut knew. Instead of saying more himself, A-wut watched Decha continue playing with the lighter, barely moving his fingers as he clicked it open and closed, making it light each time. It was ominous and hypnotizing to watch, more ominous still when Decha stopped, and they were plunged into silence again.

"So." Decha said after a long moment as he delicately wiped the lighter with his thumb and forefinger.

A-wut nodded, knowing what they'd been ordered to do. "We'll stop him."

"I hope so," Decha said, before placing a hand on A-wut's shoulder. It was menacingly heavy. "I really hope so."

"The Big Man has nothing to worry about." A-wut said, trying to keep his voice steady. He could feel the pressure of Decha's hand on his neck. He didn't move.

"And his friend," Decha added, taking his hand off A-wut's shoulder and picking up the lighter again.

A-wut tore his eyes away from Decha's penetrating stare. He watched a small girl in matching red scarf and gloves pick a strawberry from the ground and eat it. The flame appeared again.

"His friend too. Of course."

Meanwhile, in a more welcoming part of Paris, Boon had left Felix in their taxi and gone to ring the doorbell of his Aunt Vivi's house. When making plans to go to Thailand, Boon had suggested stopping in Paris. His aunt had promised to give him a gift—money, Boon presumed—from her inheritance, both for the occasion and as bait for him to come at all. They would use that money for the remaining plane tickets.

The house was smaller than they'd imagined, but incredibly ornate. From the car, Felix saw a curtain flicker and not a minute later a short woman, with bright red lip and a bob, opened the door and ran out to greet them. Vivi fussed about Boon, patting down his shirt and hair, and when Felix climbed the steps to the house, gave him polite kisses on each cheek. When she pulled back to take a *good proper look* at the boys, Felix could still smell her vanilla perfume lingering between them. He loved her instantly.

"How long will you be staying?" Vivi asked once they had brought in their bags and piled them in the hallway. The floor was some type of smooth granite that made her voice carry through the apartment.

Felix was regarding the house intently, everything very delicate and minuscule, when he replied. "Our flight leaves on Saturday."

"Saturday?" Vivi exclaimed, letting her jacket fall from her shoulders onto a chair. She had a certain tragic intensity about her. "What will you *do* in all that time?"

Before either could reply, she floated to the kitchen, signaling the two to follow with one red-lacquered hand. Twirling her fingers to warm them up, she set some water to boil over a pearly stove and went about gathering various delicacies to place on a china serving tray. Then she spoke as if she were picking up from a previous conversation. As Felix and Boon would get to know, she always had something on her mind.

"Your father needs to visit me," she said, "I can't believe he's never been to Paris. Here, pass that box of chocolates. Thanks. Never once in how many years." She popped one in her mouth as she talked, waving her hands dramatically in the air. "It's such terrible weather where you live, Boon. And to think I've *invited* your father, I'm just so lonely here." She placed another chocolate in her mouth as she worked on brewing the tea, something fragrant and pink.

The two boys settled at her kitchen table, a glass surface on three slender legs with chairs to match. A Patricia Kaas solo crooned on the radio. They held their sweaters in their laps and hugged their elbows to avoid bumping into the pretty cupboards or knocking down a flower vase or glass bowl of fruit. This kitchen was not made for men.

Still, Vivi was an expert host and assembled the tea tray quickly, leading them into a plush living room once she was finished. Stiff from the trip, Felix excused himself to the restroom to freshen up, leaving Vivi to arrange the doll-like tea on a table and Boon sinking into the most elaborate leather couch he had ever seen.

"We'll try not to miss you too much," Boon said, waving his hand at the doorway and picking up a macaroon. Vivi laughed and said something in reply, but Felix had already left.

Besides the chatting from the room, the house was quiet. There were three doors along the hallway, and after hesitating for a moment, Felix opened the first one. It wasn't the bathroom but a room the size of one, the furniture petite and low to the ground, as if a child could fit in the tiny house alongside Vivi. He had no interest in snooping, and was about to step out when a certain object caught his eye, a ceramic elephant on the bedside table, dressed in a red and gold shawl with a pattern that Felix recognized. The elephant's tail waved the Thai flag with the word *Thailand*, to leave no doubts about its origins, as if not evident enough. It was obviously a kiosk souvenir, but there was something about the tacky colors and bold little tassels of the shawl that prodded his memory.

Moving his eyes from the statuette, he found Vivi's room less personal than the tiny kitchen. Still, it was cozy. His feet sunk in the cream carpet as he walked about, smelling a pot of flowers on the windowsill. It was only when he looked up and saw a very thin, lacy nightgown that he blushed deep red and hurried back out of the door.

Back in the hallway, he could feel the blood rush to the tips of his ears. "Alright, Felix, alright." he whispered to himself.

It was the third door that opened to the bathroom. He was still blushing as he looked at himself in the mirror, his heart beating a little too hard, his lips tugged into a grin. This room cut all sounds from the house completely. He went through the motions of washing his hands more meticulously than he'd ever done, picking up a nib of pink soap with his stupidly large fingers, scraping underneath his short nails, all the way up to his wrists. Laying the towel back after drying his hands, he even squirted a dot of lotion and rubbed it in. The vanilla scent brought a fresh wave of blood to his head.

Yet something was off when he stepped out, because as he walked back down the hallway he could hear hushed voices coming from the living room. Someone had closed the french doors, the reason, Felix thought, why the house had felt so quiet. He stood behind the wall, not sure whether to go inside.

"I'll tell him." This was Boon. It wasn't hard to recognize his voice; he'd never learnt to whisper and his attempt was short of effective.

Vivi's voice, however, as suits a pro whisperer, was hard to catch, and Felix wasn't sure if she was speaking Thai, English or—*hell even French*. Nonetheless, he could hear the excitement in Boon's responses. He had a feeling that whatever was being said would end if he walked inside.

Without moving much, he twisted his shoulders in a way where he could see more of the room without giving himself away. Vivi's back was to him, Boon to her left, and they were handling something in a black bag. Boon's eyes were narrowed and focused on the bag.

Felix was about to lean further when a hand snaked in front of his mouth and another spun him around. He was face to face with a stubby young man—someone that looked vaguely familiar and, when he smirked, awfully similar to Boon.

But the man put a finger on his mouth and pushed past Felix to hover next to the door. Almost immediately his smug expression fell, and he huffed for a moment before grabbing the door handle, still holding thickly to Felix's wrist, and strode inside.

"Boon." The man's voice was surprisingly curt and nasal.

Boon turned around and cleared his throat while Vivi smoothly placed the black bag inside a cupboard, signaling that whatever they had been talking about was over.

"Felix," Boon replied, taking a sip of tea and acknowledging the stubby fingers on Felix's wrist with a frown, "that gentleman who is holding onto you like a savage, would be my Cousin George."

Then, George looked Felix up and down as if he'd only just seen him. He smiled back at Boon and Vivi, widening his eyes, before plodding himself down on the couch and placing both hands behind his head.

"Well, well," he said, drawing out the words, "What a *lovely* surprise!"

With the final ray of sunlight ebbing from the dining room, Vivi set down the last dish, gave a nod, and sat back as the three boys began helping themselves dinner from the feast that lay on the table. It was a mix of things, toasted bread with some local spreads, an Indian-style lamb, and vegetables cut in strips and seasoned with fish sauce and other Thai flavors.

"I didn't know you cooked." Boon said, taking out a cigarette from his jacket.

"I wish you'd quit that habit. Smoking makes me crazy." Vivi tapped her nails on the tablecloth a couple times, but before Boon had managed to draw the first breath, she placed a swan-shaped ashtray in front of him.

"*Everyone* smokes in Thailand. I remember you had to walk through clouds of smoke to get anywhere, and I was pregnant with him," she gestured to George without taking her eyes off the glowing tip of the cigarette. "You're going to feel *right* at home again there. I don't miss it at all. How *is* your brother, though?"

Boon switched the cigarette to his other hand and poured himself some more wine. Curiously, Felix observed, he seemed to chew through the words. "He's fine. I don't hear much from him. My parents mostly talk to him, but landline calls from Thailand cost a lot."

Vivi spooned herself some lamb and moved it around her plate with her fork. "That's right. How much older than you is he?"

"I was sixteen when we moved to New York, he was thirty one."

"He's never wanted to join you in America?"

Boon stiffened for a moment, but he shrugged and continued with the meal.

Felix's eyes narrowed. The silence was broken by George grunting and taking a loud swig of wine. He looked around the room as if searching for a fly that had been buzzing in his ear. Boon took a long draw from his cigarette.

Vivi didn't seem to notice, but she suddenly stood up and opened a window. Sitting back down again she turned to Felix and asked, "So, where *did* you go today?"

Boon and him had been out of the house all afternoon and, due to their lacking sense of direction, had spent more time weaving from street to street than seeing anything worth mentioning. Vivi was leaning on her elbows, her red lips pouted as she waited for an answer. She was the kind of woman to know her way around. Felix blushed.

"We actually spent most of our time in Place des Vosges right near here." He nodded, trying to find words to sum up their unfruitful time around the city, taking a sip of wine, weighing the pause. "The weather was fantastic."

George snickered, "You should have gone to le Jardin des Plantes. It's much more beautiful—"

"Is not!" Vivi interjected, glancing up at her son. "At this time of year the daffodils haven't even *bloomed*."

The time Boon and Felix had spent at Place des Vosges, with its stone fountains, trimmed hedges, and the building itself built by Henri IV and originally called *La Place Royale*, had been short of breathtaking. But George huffed at his mother.

"Of course they have," George continued, dismembering the cork of the wine with his meat knife, "they bloom in February."

"End of."

"Right."

"So," Vivi said, now folding a paper napkin into a swan, copying the ashtray, "they haven't bloomed yet."

"It's been a hot year."

"Felix, you were at the park, nevermind which one," she arched her eyebrows but kept her eyes on her work. "Were the daffodils blooming?"

Felix caught Boon's eye again and the corner of his lip betrayed him. "No, they weren't."

Boon smirked as a piece of cork flew from under George's thumb into George's cup, and he struggled to keep his voice even in saying, "Don't take it too harshly cousin. You were never good at arguing, even as a child. Isn't that sweet?"

George let the knife fall into the plate, making a great deal of noise that drowned his half-mumbled excuse of making coffee as he got up and exited the room. He pretended not to hear Boon snicker behind a fresh cigarette.

In the dining room, the three listened to a light jazz solo playing from a bar a little way down the street until George came back, cradling a bottle of cognac instead of coffee. With him, George brought along a lot of noise—whether grunting or heavy breathing, it was never peaceful in the room.

After sitting down once more, George cleared his throat and looked at Vivi. "Are you sure?"

She'd finished the swan and had placed it on her plate.

"No," she said, with a little smirk.

"I told you. When I went with Louise the flowers—"

"Who's Louise?" Boon said, suddenly interested.

"I don't want to bring her into—"

Boon put his hands on the table. A marketing man, he knew how to talk to people to get what he wanted. "This is the first time we have a family reunion since we were seven," he nodded toward his cousin, "I'd love to get to know you."

George hesitated, looked into the three expecting faces, and drained his glass of cognac, defeated. He poured small glasses of red wine for everyone, a slightly bigger one for himself, and flicked the radio on. "She's my girlfriend. And my mother can't stand her."

Vivi was back to leaning on her elbows, and her red lips were droopy and dramatic, but she spoke with as much conviction as ever. "That's right, I don't like that girl *at all*."

This *was* a family reunion, as Boon had noted, but Felix was invested. And to his and Boon's enjoyment, a vein in George's forehead had begun to lift since they'd mentioned Louise.

Felix probed further. "Why?"

George, unusually, seemed out of words. They listened to Édith Piaf over George's humming, until Vivi got impatient and sent him to *actually* make coffee.

"The way I want it." She called after his footsteps fading down the hall.

The moment they heard rummaging in the kitchen, Vivi sighed and dabbed at her mouth with a crisp napkin, leaving faint red marks where her lipstick smudged.

"She's not *awful*, just can't think for herself. She'd pass on a good bottle of wine because some friend of hers thinks so. I don't know how George stands that. Imagine, going out to dinner and she doesn't even know where—" she jumped out of her seat to close the window. "Sorry. It's too cold for February. *That* I miss of Phuket." she said, and then she leaned further in her seat. Her cheeks were flushed and her eyes sparkling. Felix realized she was drunk.

"Have you ever been back?" Boon asked.

"No."

All day, Felix had walked around in awe. He couldn't yet believe they'd made it out of the country, that they would see his home in less than a week. He had seen the Eiffel Tower! He smiled at the fact, breathing in the scent of smoke and candles and spices and looking out the window to the opulence outside.

"I can't wait." he said, twirling a fork on its handle.

But Vivi's expression had changed. She began to drum her fingers on the back of his chair, and exchanged a look with Boon. Felix frowned, but remained silent.

Édith sang another song before George returned. "Perfect," he grumbled, the cups teetering on the tray.

They moved the dirty plates to make room for the coffee, yet no one reached for the steaming pot until George, out of spite for his efforts, poured himself a brimming cup and sat staring at it. Close by, a church bell sounded ten strikes.

"Oh George," Vivi sighed, her gaze fixed on a stain of coffee George had spilled, "do you have to be this clumsy?" But she held her hand up before he could argue back. "Georgie, why don't you show Felix his room now?"

The radio sang louder than ever. She had been looking at Boon, who nodded back knowingly, but she turned to face George until he shifted in his chair.

"It's only ten." George said.

"They've been traveling all day."

"It's early."

There was little he could say to shake his mother though, so he heaved himself from the table and, while doing so, knocked over the empty wine bottle and spilled hot coffee from the cup he was holding all over his hand, adding to the stains on the tablecloth.

All the way down the hallway, he swore in French, something Felix found odd since they'd been speaking in Thai the whole time, and held his hand against his white shirt like a wounded soldier. Felix himself was a bit tipsy, but he could hear George growling about making coffee if no one was going to drink it. Besides that, he said no words to Felix.

They walked across the apartment, where they reached a door that George had to put his weight against to open. Inside, he breezed past the room and led Felix onto the balcony, where they stood side by side facing the municipal swimming pool, with its water-stained walls and rusty banisters. Felix had assumed George would say something now, but he stood quiet, leaning with both hands on the frail railing and puffing in the cold air.

"So have you ever been to New York?" Felix said, tapping the railing with the tip of his shoe.

George frowned and heaved himself straight. Even with his chest puffed high, he was rather stocky and Felix rose past him easily. "You smoke?"

"Uh, no." Felix said, "Boon does."

"Right, of course." He had been reaching inside his jacket for, presumably, a smoke, but he now smoothed it down instead. He glared at Felix. They listened to about ten cars pass on the street below.

"In the morning don't open the windows."

"What?"

George made a show of having to repeat himself. He was still upset about the smoke, and more precisely, about Vivi shooing him out of his own dining room—he wanted to make someone *else* miserable. After explaining it again, he wiped his face with a heavy arm, and with it, a smirk.

"You sure you don't want to?" he said, crossing his arms in front of his chest, one hand ready with the lighter.

But Felix was, in fact, tired, and the two soon headed inside. On the street, a cat scurried across the front of a butchery both ways before sitting on its front step. George gestured vaguely at the cabinets and mumbled something about blankets and pillows and was out of the room before Felix could ask any questions.

"What are we going to do?"

Prompt at five, Felix had woken up to the screeching of metal rubbing over metal and the smell of Paris' trash right under their open window. He'd gotten up and had been pacing next to it since. The sky was still dark as Boon pressed his palms against his eyes and took a sip of water. Felix took the glass and held it to his temples. Even with the wintry February air cutting through his clothes, the room felt tight.

"So this is the big thing she wanted to give you."

"Yes.

"Alright." Felix's voice rose for a second. The two were hissing to each other to avoid waking anyone else up, or more importantly be heard. The word clung to his throat.

"There was never any money, Felix. This," he said, picking up the small figurine, "was the inheritance she wanted to give me. I'm sorry."

"And that's that?" but he coiled up onto the armchair, rested his chin on his knee and went quiet.

Aunt Vivi had gifted Boon a bejeweled chameleon. Framed with delicate rose-gold wire which curled intricately at the toes and tongue, it stood on three legs and extended one toward the open window. The skin, a tapestry of small jade and emerald gems, glittered in the semi-darkness of their room.

"We could sell it."

"Boon—"

"I'm serious. There's bound to be antique collectors here in Paris that would buy it from us, that or exchange shops or pawn shops. It's a pretty little thing, and absolutely smashed by jewels. You know better than me, we need this money to get to Thailand."

"Boon." The two friends looked at each other and Felix gave a short smile. "You know you don't have to sell it if you don't want to."

"Of course I want to sell it." Boon laughed and rubbed his knuckles together. From the way his smile lingered Felix could tell he was serious. "Felix, I just hate that we have to pawn it in the first place. I couldn't care less for this." With that he put on his jacket and pocketed the animal. Amusement still played around his features, tugging his mouth in an uneven smirk. "Felix, we're going to get the money and go to Thailand and this chameleon will be snug inside someone else's jacket soon."

Only then, they started getting ready for the day. Outside, an old lady was pulling up the shutters of a *boulangerie* while a line of heavy-breasted mothers chatted at the bus stop, and a row of bicycles passed by. Children with pink and green backpacks were bobbing across the street as a policeman stopped a white Peugeot from crossing at the same time, and, a little further away from all this, was an older man with a camera, setting up a tripod and a lens to capture the side of the old swimming pool, with the rusted railings and water-splotched walls, and the icy-blue sky. In a city like Paris, their savior could be anyone.

Chapter 6

DEEP IN THE NINETEENTH ARRONDISSEMENT, squeezed between two buildings postered with "for sale" signs, the alley reeked of something corrosive. It's funny how some people love their jobs, Baptiste thought as he secured the shutters and opened the door to the warmth inside his shop. Behind him, the alley was caked in the remains of garbage and stray cats, overdue for a bleaching by the Sanitation Department. The shop itself didn't smell good, partly due to the golden oil lamp Baptiste had just traded, which even after having been polished and locked behind thick glass, filled the room with a distasteful coppery smell of rust. Baptiste wasn't old, but his bad hip made it a struggle to settle into his leather desk chair without spilling the coffee he was holding. Normally, he'd stop at the *Café Valentin* on the way to work, but the morning had started off cold, so he had talked with Nick, the bartender, only for a couple of minutes, and grabbed the earlier bus instead.

He was flipping through the fourth magazine of the day when Felix and Boon walked in, and he glared at the two. If there was anything he hated, it was young boys walking into his shop, because he knew they could only be there for one reason. His eyes followed their hands with scrutiny.

The very first thing he'd pickpocketed himself was a wallet on Rue La Gare when he was fourteen. In 1972, between the eighteenth and nineteenth arrondissements, people traded in cigarettes and settled fights with knives—no one was stupid enough to carry cash. So he'd learnt to pickpocket from Tousche, that was what they all called him. He had sent all the *petites* in different areas of the city, and taught them how to bump against someone and slip a hand, white-gloved, into a pocket or a handbag. That one morning, Tousche had stolen close to three hundred francs from a woman's wallet and bought them all lemon popsicles. He was, quite rightly, the boss.

Baptiste thought back to the man he had first stolen from. Most of the younger guys had been hesitant to really go for it —they leaned cautiously against pretty storefronts with hands low in their coats, trying to look tough, hoping for an easy mark. He, however, had chosen a prime location just behind a bus shed. He would've rather pickpocketed the women, who tended to be more distracted in that area of Paris and therefore easier targets, but there weren't any around. Instead, after a bit of waiting, he saw a stubby Irish man. About his own height, he sported a large beer belly and wore an ill-fitting blazer. Locking eyes with Tousche for a second, Baptiste spun out of his hiding spot, ran shoulder-first into the man, thrust his hand into the jacket's inside pocket, curled his fingers over the ma's wallet and smoothly moved it into his own coat as he stepped to the side and half-apologized before heading off. He'd scored big, with a whole fifty francs and a birthday card that sang a fun song when he opened it. From then, he'd been nicknamed *Nez Fin*, for his ability to smell out a fat stash of money.

Watching the two young men enter his shop, he sensed something different about them. It might've been their nervousness, which wasn't the nervousness of a thief or a kid about to try a snatch and run. Or perhaps it was the uncertainty with which their eyes glossed over the glass cases and golden watches, because if Baptiste could smell out anything, clearly and easily, it was the smell of indecision.

"Est-ce que je peux vous aider?" He looked at them over the rim of his wire-framed glasses without putting the magazine down.

"Mais…oui, s'il vous plaît." Felix had studied French in high school, and although he didn't think that his knowledge of adjectives and animals would be of much help in this situation, he was excited to finally put it to the test. Baptiste scowled and lowered his glasses on his nose. Boon tried English instead.

"We need to exchange an item of value." As he said this, Boon leaned forward, placing the tips of his fingers on the counter, as if to emphasize his Americanness. "You speak English, yes?" he added, pointing to a sign on the wall a drunk Englishman might have written as a joke.

Baptiste narrowed his eyes. "A little bit. So what's the item?"

"It's an antique and we want a fair price. We won't trade it otherwise." And with this Boon placed the small chameleon on the glass counter.

Dilettantes, Baptiste thought, reaching for his glasses, but his eyes were hungry. He picked up the figurine and held it up to the light so the jewels could catch it just right. Small green dots danced all over his hands. He spoke with as much nonchalance as he could.

"Thirty, thirty-five," he tilted his head back and grazed a finger over the shell, "maybe forty."

"Thousands?" Boon said, unable to mask his surprise.

"Oui." Baptiste said, and hearing the boy's response, repeated the lower number, "Thirty-five thousand francs."

"Francs?" Boon stopped for a moment, "Are you kidding me? That's just a little over six thousand dollars. Is this a joke?"

"I'm afraid not, monsieur. It's quite a fine little thing, *oui*, but it poses quite a risk, don't you think? I don't keep anything in here worth more than ten thousand dollars anyway."

"It's worth at least ten! It's embedded in emeralds for chrissake! In fact, it's worth well above ten, it's an original Pascale Monvoisin made here, in France."

"I think you're mistaking emerald for jade, *monsieur*."

"C'est ainsi que vous traitez les clients?" It was the only phrase Boon had learned from his job in marketing, and usually, it was directed at him.

Turning from the counter, Boon said under his breath, "Felix, what are we gonna do? We need the money."

"I know."

"We need—" Boon paused, rubbing his face in his hands, "it's not even mine, per se."

"*Que?*"

They spun back around to find the short man glowering at them.

"I do not buy *stolen* things. I'm not in that market." The second was a bit of a lie, as was the first. From where he stood, Baptiste could see a handful of things bought under the table.

"It's not stolen. It's a gift from his aunt." Felix watched as Boon raked his fingers through his hair. They shared a glance before Boon nodded.

"Alright. How much would you give us?"

"Thirty."

"But you said forty earlier. And anyway we won't sell for less than ten thousand dollars."

"I said maybe. I'll give you thirty-five thousand francs for it." Baptiste put his hands in his pockets, still seemingly uninterested.

Having a strong sense that the man was screwing them, Felix turned to Boon. "You know what? This is wrong anyway. You shouldn't sell a gift from your aunt. Let's get out of here."

Boon got the memo. Putting the figurine back in his pocket they started walking towards the entrance. When they were almost there, Baptiste, trying to mask his desire, gave a big yawn, ripping a hole in his left pocket as his hand pushed through.

"Forty thousand, no more."

After some hesitation, Boon reluctantly agreed. A moment later the chameleon stood poised on the glass, its tail seeming to curl on forever as Baptiste counted the money and opened a dark, velvety box to store it in. It was hypnotizing to watch the light reflecting from the gold and so many jewels, so Felix began to glance about himself for the first time since they'd stepped in the shop. Apart from the bad smell, he'd expected the insides to be less clean and more iron-bars and leather jackets, more weapons on the walls.

"I'll tell you what," said Baptiste, feeling a warm sense of self-congratulation as he organized the bills in his cash drawer and wrote up a receipt, "forty, plus this." And with that he produced a small package wrapped in old newspaper held by a thick black ribbon. The box wasn't fancy, just an ordinary wooden box fitted with a latch at the front. Opening the box, Baptiste slowly took out a small wooden statue in the shape of a baby angel (or demon—it was hard to say). Standing with wings half-spread, feet oddly sprawled, eyes wide and contemptuous, it was the ugliest statue Felix had ever seen.

"Please put it away," Boon said, grimacing at the angel's face over the top of the box.

They had been sitting at the same bar for about an hour, in which, periodically, Felix would pull out the statue to feel the jagged carvings with his thumb, and Boon would avert his eyes and order another shot of *Picon* for both of them. After about five glasses everything began smelling of the orange-flavored liquor, so Boon began ordering wine instead. Paris was, after all, the romantic wine cellar of Europe.

"We got a statuette."

Felix hadn't gotten over the deal yet and was still trying to discern the fact that, after as many beers and ways he would look at the thing, there wasn't one good look about it. He missed the chameleon's tongue. It curled in such a perfect circle.

"At least we have the money," Boon said, patting his jacket.

"We sure do."

"More drinks?"

"Please."

The bartender was a man in his forties, with bleached hair and a habit of winking his left eye. A respectable man and an experienced bartender—a jack of all trades who juggled glass bottles and made origami swans out of women's brochures— he was someone the regulars would call *a real nice guy*. He was however feeling a sense of conflict: when two young men were paying seventy francs for every drink, it was damn hard to advise them to stop.

It was three in the morning by the time they stumbled off the stools and onto the cobbled street with the statue in its box. During the fourth game of billiard, Boon had taken his shoes off and Felix had stuffed his tie in another man's coat. Disheveled and drunk, they hoped the cold air would sober them up a bit. It was a particularly biting night, and they were in shirtsleeves. Boon had forgotten to retrieve his shoes, but didn't feel like going back inside. Shivering, they stood on the sidewalk looking around, thinking the other was deciding what to do next.

"I've never seen the moon so close before." Boon said finally, looking up at a lamppost. "Felix, come look, quick before it goes away."

"You just don't *get* this in New York."

"Do you miss it?"

"Already?" Felix rubbed his eyes, burned by the light, "A little. Not really."

Boon also looked down, squinting his eyes until his head started to turn. Opening them, he noticed a wine stain on his collar that he tried to suck up before deciding to throw the shirt away. He saw that Felix was yawning.

"Let's go home."

They waited at an intersection for the light to turn green twice before realizing they could cross. At first, neither talked. Felix was busy swinging his arms freely by his sides, while

Boon was trying not to hobble on the coarse cement that made up the road. With the city only half illuminated, they kept their eyes peeled to the ground to avoid tripping, missing, in the meantime, the graffiti on the side of buildings, unlit Easter bunny decorations hanging on lampposts, and the Eiffel Tower, itself uncharacteristically dark against the sky.

Usually, the tenth arrondissement of Paris was beautiful in spring—with its elm-lined bridges, canals, and pianists in waistcoats smoking outside of grand hotels. But at night, frost on every bench and drunk men prowling the streets for a place to crash was entirely less safe, especially as they neared the nineteenth arrondissement.

It was a while before the growing danger occurred to Felix. "Where are we going?" he said, looking around himself.

Boon kept on walking, his head bobbing slightly up and down with each sluggish step. Felix felt a wave of nausea.

"Boon."

"I thought you knew," his friend said, reaching a set of stairs and sitting down.

"Everything's in French." Felix noted, squinting at a sign and grimacing. "I don't know what *anything* means."

"Well I can't feel my feet." Boon said, reaching down to squeeze his toes. He looked at Felix and shook his head. "No, I'm serious."

Felix placed his hands over his ears, red from the cold, and looked up at the sky. Boon bent his toes until they cracked. His eyes shot open. He then noticed a ten franc coin on the step, picked it up and held it up close to his eyes.

"So which way now?" Felix asked, slowly feeling his own feet go numb.

But Boon shrugged and continued looking at his coin. Boon had always had an eye for things, especially in New York, when every two steps there was something shiny and unnoticed in the cracks of the pavement. One time, when they were thirteen and sixteen, Boon had found a whole pouch of dollar coins hidden behind a gnarly tree root at Central Park. It was only when they tried to buy a secondhand football from the local thrift that they realized the coins were forged. Felix chuckled to himself, wondering what had come of them.

"What?" Boon asked, finally looking up at Felix.

"Where should we go?"

They were standing in front of an old theater advertising the opening of *The Wizard of Oz!* in two weeks. Felix's teeth were chattering as he moved toward Boon, but he spun on his heels before extending a hand and pulling his friend up on his feet. Lips stiff from the cold, he glanced back to the poster, where Dorothy was pointing straight ahead of them, and then began skipping in that direction.

"I think the Louvre is this way." he said, and together, they made their way across the city on an imaginary golden road.

It was a while before they stopped again. Immediately Boon sat on the pavement, holding his feet, while Felix pulled one knee up to his chest at a time to keep warm. At different intersections they'd flipped the coin to decide where to go, walking down one unpromising road after another. Felix now nodded toward a cardboard box marked with the words "Keep out" hidden in a doorway.

"I don't like this," he said.

They'd been singing songs to keep themselves entertained, and Boon ignored Felix to hum the chorus of one.

Felix chuckled tentatively, but he looked over his shoulder at the dark nooks between buildings. "We need a map. There are no goddamn maps in this city." He couldn't tell if something was moving in one of the doorways.

Boon was nodding his head along to some beat, and continued even when Felix shuffled closer. "What?"

"There aren't any maps around here," Felix repeated.

"You're right."

"How are people supposed to get places?"

"I don't know." Boon said, going back to the tune.

Felix stamped his foot on the ground to get some blood flowing, and crossed his arms.

Boon looked up. "No, I mean, it sucks—"

"Can you quit singing and help me get us home? I'm tired as hell."

Boon stopped humming. Standing up slowly, he groaned, saying "I'm so damn cold, I feel like my legs are about to fall off."

Felix swayed in the dark and cold. He'd spent the whole journey trying so hard to think clearly and remember his way around that he now had a headache. He squeezed his temples and winced when his icy fingers made contact.

Twice now, they'd been lost in Paris. While in New York, he thought, it was easy to tell which of two roads was the least foreboding, Paris deceived them with its vintage, rustic charm, so by the time they found themselves in that alley, in the middle of the nineteenth arrondissement, it was too late. They had been right to sing, because without it, somehow, the darkness was more pronounced. Something scurried behind Felix. He was trying to rub the Picon out of his head when he felt Boon's sharp elbow make contact with his ribs. Boon's other hand was stretched out in front of him, wobbling but fixed on a particular shadow. Felix had to shake his head a couple of times before focusing on the varying depths of black, and seeing, in the gloom cast by an old church, the silhouette of a man.

The two boys looked at each other and then back at the figure.

"Should we walk past him?" Felix whispered.

"I don't know," Boon said back, Felix wincing at the noise. "No, let's return to the bar or something."

But the two had only taken a couple of steps back, when the man lunged forward.

"Arretez eh!"

While the shout had startled them, Felix holding the statuette tighter and Boon jumping in his spot, there was something about the tone that they recognized.

"Arretez lá." the man repeated, moving to another patch of near-light, closer to them.

The two narrowed their eyes and looked at each other. The man began clicking something metallic, so that with everything else silent, they could almost hear the spring draw breath each time.

"Mets tes mains sur ton épaules," he said, louder when neither of them moved, "Oilá, mets tes mains sur ton épaules."

Felix was running his thumb over the latch of the box, trying to figure out what the man wanted, when the church struck the half hour. With a look at Boon, he realized he had no idea of how long they had walked for. As they listened to the chimes and watched a pigeon fly from the roof of a house to another, Felix repeated the phrase in his head.

"What was that?" he whispered to Boon, "Met the men, Tom and Paul?"

Boon shook his head slowly. "I've got no idea."

The man was leaning casually on a postbox, or perhaps the postbox leaned on him. He started talking to them again, though neither could understand.

"Doesn't it," Boon started, lowering his voice when Felix nudged him in the ribs, "doesn't it sound like George?"

Felix held his breath and tried to distinguish the voice, but he struggled to focus. He closed his eyes and opened them again when he began to lose his balance. "I don't know. Could be."

Because the man had slipped into another pool of shadow, they hadn't seen him approach. He'd started to sweat. It was cold sweating, icy perspiration—he was flicking his lighter on and off to keep his fingertips from freezing. To stop the cold getting to his nose he had been breathing into his coat, but now, moist with condensation, the wet lip of the collar stuck to his neck uncomfortably.

Boon and Felix had stopped listening to him, and jumped again when he stepped into the half-light, a couple steps from them.

"Hey!" Felix said, flinching slightly when he caught sight of the figure, "what—"

"Listen here," the man said, pulling his hat low on his eyes and his neck in his coat. He was stubby up close, like a cigar put out after a bad business meeting. "You're going to put your hands on your head and hand me the satchel." He inched toward them.

Boon spoke tentatively. "Cousin George?"

The man took a large gulp of air before sliding into a nearby shadow. "To hell with these distractions. Now hand over the money." The line sounded rehearsed, but his voice darkened.

It was early in the morning, the hours stretched as thin as the bottom of Boon's left sock. Had they walked in the right direction, they would have seen the early dawn reflecting in the Louvre's glass, trickling to life over the bridges. But they hadn't, and Felix shivered again. The sky seemed to pulse black the more he looked at it.

"Money? What money?" Boon's tone had changed too, but his eyes fluttered. Gradually, it seemed he was fighting to keep them on the man.

"Where is it?"

"I don't—"

"Dammit," the man said, and with that he hit Boon's jaw, grabbed the strap of Boon's satchel, the one he carried for wallets, passports and other valuables, and slung it across his own body.

Taken by surprise, Boon was too tired and uncoordinated to fight back.

"Tu tais." the man snapped at Felix.

By now the sun was beginning to come up, even if feeble and sickly in his part of town. The man looked at the satchel, the thick leather smooth and heavy. He gave a last glance at Felix, whose mouth was open and puffing steam, and Boon, whose jaw already gave signs of bruising over, gave a final smirk, and ran.

Chapter 7

"GODDAMNIT A-WUT."

It was the fifth time he had shone the flashlight in Decha's eyes since they had begun to work on breaking the shop's lock. A-wut had done nothing useful so far except get his body in the way of the light and drop a small wrench on Decha's forehead.

"I need it *on my hands*. Here, no. Alright, now hold it still." Decha said, grabbing a lock pick rake from his pocket and maneuvering it in the keyhole. He fiddled with it for a couple of minutes before dropping it on the floor and grabbing a bigger one. "All these goddamn locks—"

With eight locks of different measure, type, and technology, the pawn shop was more secure than Bastille. They were taking more time than Decha would have liked, but the street was empty. Darker than most nights, the sky hung silent and huge over Paris. This was A-wut's first time in France—he found the tall buildings and cramped alleys reassuring, good for spying.

He and Decha had identified the boy, Felix, and his friend that morning, and had managed to catch them entering the pawn shop without being seen. A-wut had called the Big Man from a nearby tabac, spending an unreasonable amount of francs to listen to his boss grunt into the phone and hang up. Felix was up to something, they were sure. Whatever business he had in a pawn shop might help them understand his connection to the Big Man.

"If this doesn't work," Decha said, holding his breath as he jammed his last pick against the tension wrench in the ancient mechanism and wriggled the instruments about. A-wut held his breath. It was another cold night. Walking to the pawn shop, the slight layer of frosted dew had crinkled beneath their feet. The moment the pins caught and the latch sprung open echoed in the narrow alley. Decha kneeled to pick up the discarded tools and stuffed them in his bag, while A-wut dug his fingernails into the handle of the flashlight and cringed at the noise.

"Decha—"

"What?" He whispered, whipping his head around and dropping a metal nail in the meantime, causing A-wut to flinch, "Instead of standing there, why don't you try the door, *ngî ngèā?*"

A-wut placed his hand on the door handle and sighed. "Decha, our biggest problem is the alarms."

"It's alright."

"How—"

But Decha had stood up, placed his own hand on the knob, over A-wuts, and with a heavy lunge into his companion, his shoulder pushing the door open, they stumbled into the shop.

A-wut had tensed and fell into a glass case, sending an ornamental Chinese dhow onto the floor. Decha, instead, steadied himself, moved toward a painting by the door, swung it outward and flicked a switch. He counted seven seconds on his watch. A-wut waited quietly—he narrowed his eyes when nothing happened.

"I watched the owner earlier. He closed the shop and then snuck in from the back to set the alarm." He pointed toward the painting, "Such a simple one for that."

A-wut checked his own watch and his jaw hardened. "C'mon, let's look around and get out."

They started on opposite sides of the shop, A-wut filing through papers and receipts and Decha perusing the isles at the back. He strutted between the glass cases, peering into vases, plucking guitar strings, spinning the wheel of a hanging bike, wearing a smug smile. "Such a simple alarm," he repeated, chuckling to himself.

A-wut was working on a locked drawer when he smelled the cigar. He remained hunched, fiddling with his tools, until the lock clicked. Then, he looked over the counter and spotted the orange tip glowing in the half-light.

"Decha!" he hissed across the room. "For christsake, stop it right—"

"Have you found anything yet?" Decha demanded. He disliked being bossed around and stretched his neck both ways to calm himself. "Have you?" he asked, his eyes intent on a case of weapons.

A-wut hadn't yet looked inside the drawer. "Just some receipts. A lot of bills. Seriously, the fire alarm will go off. If you—"

"Keep looking."

"I have been, what about—"

"I want us to be in and out okay? Let's not waste time." With that, Decha ducked behind a commendable display of watches, the orange dot dancing behind the glass as he chewed on the other end.

A-wut's nostrils flared, but he went back to work. Some light filtered from the streetlights into the shop, but he held the flashlight in his mouth to see better. Surprisingly, the drawer was very neat. He didn't know why he had assumed the opposite. In a pile were the most recent sales, and in another, the exchanges. He shuffled through the top few papers, scanning the handwritten notes, stopping when he found a receipt issued at the time when Felix had visited.

Working in black markets had taught him one thing: the least amount of information was the safest. A-wut wasn't surprised at how sparse the receipt was. Just an amount of francs, a first name, and less often than not, what was traded. Felix had both sold and bought something here, but what exactly A-wut couldn't tell. *Antiques*, A-wut read in the loopy calligraphy, thankful he knew the word, followed by something else. He stuffed the papers in his jacket so he could translate them later at their hotel.

It took him a while to find Decha. The shop wasn't very big, but had a couple of rooms in the back filled with inventory. Decha was sitting on a chair in one of them peering into a diamond ring. A drawer of similar items was open next to him.

"Anything?" he said, without looking up.

"Yes," A-wut replied, "the kid exchanged something not worth a lot of money. He also bought something antique but I don't know for how much—"

"What did he buy?"

"I don't know."

Decha nodded. He stroked the diamond with his thumb.

"This was a waste of time." A-wut said, sighing. He'd had reservations about the whole goose-chase the Big Man had them on, but he kept that to himself.

Decha nodded again, but he said, "No, no. You did well," before pulling from his cigar and tapping the ashes on the floor. "Look," he continued, "so many bright things."

A-wut had, in fact, been looking. The lights were on in the room and the jewels shone brilliantly against each other. Rings, earrings, necklaces, bracelets, cufflinks. None of the jewels were much bigger than his thumbnail, but in the collective, A-wut had never been among so much wealth.

"Some of this stuff is original, well-made," he replied.

Decha raised his eyes to his companion. "Valuable."

It was in moments like these, with Decha smoking and A-wut restless, both tired of each other, that they made the worst decisions.

"Ten minutes?" Decha asked, but A-wut had already gone to work.

Initially, they placed the smaller items, like jewelry, into their coats. Hundreds of thousands worth of stuff. A collector's dream. They broke the glass display of watches and pocketed the most luxurious ones, big names like *Rolex, Cartier,* and *Hublot*. By the time the two reached the bigger stuff, gold African artifacts, ivory and jade and lapis trinkets, they'd run out of space to carry them.

But Decha was rarely out of ideas. "Take your jacket off," he told A-wut, and there he started piling in objects.

A-wut moved to the next display containing other expensive items, and placed as many things he could in his pants pockets, a silver hip flask, gold medallions, a jeweled chameleon—

"A few more things," Decha whispered, smashing a display case and digging through the glass shards.

The store, which had been well organized and kept, was now hard to navigate though because of all the glass and discarded items on the floor. Having no more room in his pockets, A-wut moved to the counter and broke the register free from its two locks and keycode using a crowbar. It hadn't been five seconds yet, however, when a screeching siren went off.

"Goddamnit!" A-wut shouted, and pressed handfuls of bills into his shirt as Decha made his way to the front of the store again.

"What did you do?" Decha said, smashing his cigar into the counter, leaving a burn mark.

"Let's get out of—"

"I'm grabbing your coat. Hang on."

He was halfway there when A-wut reached him and pulled him back. "Let's go."

"All the stuff—"

"There's no time. You'll never be able to carry all those things anyway." He let go of Decha and strode to the door. "It's been twenty seconds."

The two slipped out of the shop and along the icy cobblestones all the way to the main road without talking. The smell of dust and rot from the store and alley hung to them as they sped away, Decha holding a single watch and A-wut struggling with his loaded pockets. It would be a while before the police would decide to investigate. The sun was just peeking through the clouds.

Somewhere, some blocks further north than the shop, past a post office and a bakery with early Easter decorations, through a couple of parks and on the side of the canal, drunk and frozen with cold, Felix thought he heard sirens. He was surprised by how many police cars got busy just because a couple of American tourists got mugged: *Paris must be made of some good stuff, after all.*

Chapter 8

HUNCHED AND GNAWING AT A pretzel the way a beaver might chomp on a block of wood, George sat tense. The bar was a dimly lit hole in the wall that he'd stumbled in soon after leaving Felix and Boon in the street. He'd only really jogged about two blocks before hearing sirens and deciding it best to lay low, ducking into the first bar still open to have a beer for his nerves. At that hour, there were only a couple old men playing cards, with features so sunk back into their faces it reminded George of pincushions, and a mutt sleeping next to an electrical heater, old as the oldest of the men.

He heard the police heading in the opposite direction of the alley and was relieved to find that the Parisian forces weren't as organized as he had feared. Still, he decided to rest for a while, and with the night's events behind him, took a pause from chewing to look around himself.

Besides the coffee, which had had the intended effect of calming him, the bar offered little warmth. An elk head was nailed to one of the walls, crazed and not too unlike Hercules.

Time stiffened the joints of the room, years tucked in the groaning seats of the chairs and door hinges. One of the men yawned then, his jaw slack as it retreated back into place. George turned back to his own. The pretzel now, stale to begin with, felt like wet sawdust in his mouth. He scratched his belly as he pondered for a moment.

With the bar so quiet, he decided to pull out the satchel he'd taken from Boon and look inside. It was heavier than he'd expected. The first thing he opened was an envelope folded unevenly down the middle. He suppressed a gasp as he leafed through its contents delicately, using his large fingers to move the stacked bills, grunting loudly when he finished counting the lot. Weary that anyone would see the money he placed it back in the bag.

It hadn't been his plan to steal their whole satchel. In fact, it had been bulky and awkward to carry when he escaped, a reason, alongside his protruding belly and flat feet, that he had not run far at all. He was still in the nineteenth arrondissement, the youngest in the bar, and to think of it made him shudder. Glancing back to the old men and noticing at least two beers on their table, he motioned to the bartender to make him an Irish coffee. If anything, he deserved a little bit of cheering up.

Waiting for his drink, he opened one of the passports. While his face hadn't exactly been joyful, it fell seeing his cousin looking up with his smug New-Yorkness. Having forgotten about the mouthful of pretzel, he felt it slide like a wet slug down his throat. After a sip of coffee, he did have a good laugh—a sort of wet low rumble—at the name *Boon-Mee*. Printed in blocky, formal letters, it reminded him of a sheep's bleat. The first and only other time the two had spent any considerable amount of time together had been when George had been eleven and he'd given Boon the nickname "Goaty." With his long, wispy hair that fell over his eyes and flat nose, George had another laugh at the passport.

If he had had any intention of running home after the quick stop, it was now gone. He realized with a half-smile that, while he wasn't drunk, he was feeling nicely warmed by the whiskey. Outside, it had started raining, the sun gone, and for a while he watched the pavements gloss over in the grayish light of the morning. Then, without much thought, he reached over the counter, grabbed a black pen, and started drawing a goatee over Boon's face.

He barely noticed two men entering the bar. They were dressed in heavy clothes and wearing dark faces—one had a particularly sour expression, with a ghost of a bruise appearing on his face, all the way from his eyebrows down to a freshly lit Cuban. Alongside them came a wave of cold that rattled the francs George had pulled out of the envelope to order himself another Irish coffee. Without many options to choose from, the men sat down next to George.

Growing up in Paris, George had seen more cigarette butts than people's faces while walking on the street, he was even proud of it. But he didn't often meet other Asians in his parts of Paris—besides his mother, he didn't know any Thai people. Trying to look like he was getting something from his coat, he flicked his eyes toward them.

The shorter of the two sported a thin mustache that ran too long on his upper lip, resembling a rat's tail or something dirty of the sort. The other man, the one closest to him, had a hard stare as he caught George's eye immediately. They exchanged quick nods and the most fleeting smiles. At first, from what he could sense without looking, they seemed to be in a tense conversation—Ratmouth shuffling something in his hands, Cuban shaking his head. It'd be moments before they would unwind into the stools, motion to the bartender and order a drink themselves. George returned to the pretzel.

Bored with Boon, he opened Felix's passport, but he didn't have much interest in it. He let the pretzel hold the page open as he sipped on the hot brew and considered the night again. So many things had happened—

He grunted when he felt something bump against his shoulder. Looking up, he found the men on either side of him.

"Can I help you?" A prick himself, George had started with a growl, but then, with their dark faces next to his, thought better of it. "Gentlemen?"

The men hesitated, obviously struggling with the French, and decided to continue in English.

"That passport you're holding," Cuban said, also making an attempt to be pleasant, "could I see it?"

"Why?"

Ratmouth gave a little snort, an ugly sound. "We know the guy."

"I do too." George spit back. If Cuban had caught on to the sarcasm, he didn't show it. "I'll let him know about this little encounter the next time I see him."

At first George had been curious about the two, but now he just wanted to finish his drink and order another one in peace.

"May I ask, why do you have another man's passport?" Cuban said, not moving an inch.

George raised his eyebrows, as if to say, *some people these days*, and continued with the same tone. "I stole it."

Ratmouth raised his own bristly eyebrows. "Stole?"

"It's an expression. Now if you *excuse me*." George said, sipping his coffee, but he felt a chill run up his spine. He bit his tongue as he waited for the men to leave.

Cuban's English was accented with something emphatic. He stood tall behind George, close enough to whisper something and be heard. By and large, George was very well wishing he was out in the rain on his way home. Still, the men didn't move.

"Look, are you the police or something? What do you want from me?"

"Be a pal, now. I told you, we know the guy."

George didn't buy this, even after a few stiff drinks. Felix —or for that matter, Boon—were like some acorns on the side of the road in Paris. In the city, people only knew him from work at the bank and through Vivi. Occasionally, he was recognized by a few people at the bar. Those two spoofs from New York couldn't have been known by anyone here. "Sure you do."

"Look here, Frenchie," and Ratmouth pulled out his own tattered wallet, "we're no cops alright? Just two men looking for our friends."

George couldn't make out if the name, A-wut, was a mistake or not his name at all, but he let out a short breath regardless. There wasn't a badge of any sort. In fact, he saw a few pictures of a little girl poking out of various pockets who, unfortunately for her, had the same scrawny black hair as Ratmouth. George let out an uncomfortable laugh.

"Then why don't you two have a drink with me and we can catch up over these friends of ours, *messieurs*?"

If he couldn't get rid of them then he would wait till they gave up, and in the meantime he had to even out the playing field. George, who usually didn't have many moments of brilliance, thought this was one of them, and, as he waited for them to sit down, slipped the passports back into the pouch.

They did two rounds of Irish coffee before Cuban finally spoke. "How do you know our friend Felix?"

"I don't really." George said, cautiously.

Ratmouth shot a look at Cuban, something George didn't like.

"I mean, I've only known him recently. You?"

"We go way back."

George didn't like this either, for he guessed it was a lie, and ordered a round of bloody marys, just for them. He felt disadvantaged against the two sober men.

"Ah, very good, very good." Cuban said offhandedly.

After a pause they ordered the same for him. He glanced at his watch.

"Look, we're here in passing. We just wondered if it's actually him."

"It is. It's his passport."

Ratmouth had, for the most part, let Cuban talk, but he cocked his head and peered at George. "You didn't actually steal it, did you?"

George, who'd been drinking the bloody mary, choked. The acid burned in his throat. "Of course it was a joke."

"If it wasn't we'd have to report you—"

"No, no. I'm Felix's friend's cousin. I work at the bank. They had to get something notarized and I'm doing them a favor."

"Of course. How kind of you." Cuban said, shooting a glance at Ratmouth and nodding. "That's very considerate."

"Let's have another coffee," said Ratmouth, ordering another round, so that even the pincushion men looked up from their chins at the growing collection of glassware on the counter. George had to be careful picking up his fresh drink.

"It's lovely."

"Whiskey."

"Right."

"Right."

Just then, Cuban whispered something to his companion that George didn't quite catch, and another drink appeared in front of him. The two men pressed on his sides, pulling the conversation this way and that while the counter filled up with drinks and empty glasses.

"What's the time?" George spat out suddenly, remembering it was a weekday.

Cuban sat up and said a number without checking his watch. George's eyes widened, and he started fumbling to get his coat on. As he was putting his hand in the second sleeve, Cuban jammed his elbow in the stool, causing George to slip off and knock a fresh drink into himself. In the confusion of the glass falling and breaking on the floor, the old men looking up, and George shouting as the hot liquid seeped into his clothes, Ratmouth snatched the satchel from the counter and placed it around his neck.

"Excuse me, *excuse me!*" George said, pushing past them on route to the bathroom, his skin burning where the drink had fallen.

He couldn't have imagined, with his eyes closed against the bright lights on the tiles, listening to the hum of pipes and the water running cold over his hands, that Cuban and Ratmouth had even helped the bartender gather the broken glass before finally grinning and slipping the two passports and money from the pouch into their pockets. While he sighed, peeling off the wet shirt from his stomach and using a soft towel to dry himself, he wasn't thinking how they might've drained their glasses, stumbled off the stools themselves, turned up the collars of their coats and stepped into the cold rain. Or how they could've headed anywhere in the immensity of Paris with their thick accent like a boat's stern off to sea, and how, when he would get back, he'd find the whole bill of drinks to pay himself. He couldn't think of anything while he looked at his bloodshot eyes in the mirror, besides calling in sick for the day and going home.

Chapter 9

EVERYTHING FROM THE PISTONS, TO the cylinders bobbing up and down, to the coal chimney, was coated in delicate gold. The main frame of the train, also metal, was a deep pine green, while the wheels, thirty or so splendid little circles in a row, caught all the specks of light that came in through the window. The toy store was just a door down from the Embassy and as the train huffed and puffed blue smoke behind the glass, Felix couldn't help but think of the New York Railroad Museum, models complete with passengers and luggage waiting to depart.

He had woken up hungover to the shock of their missing passport pouch, and had called on Vivi and a bottle of aspirin immediately. When they first arrived to Paris, Boon had explained that she was somewhat of a prominent member of the French bureaucracy (what exactly she did escaped Felix in their conversations, but he imagined that she worked her charm and avoided most due explanations), which was why she was able to pass them for emergency passports from

Washington, taking not six weeks but a single day. After their photos had been taken and some forms filled in at the embassy, they had been told to wait an hour, which was how Felix had ended up admiring the miniature Alpine locomotive on its voyage around the toy shop next door.

It was another terrible day in Paris. Windy, rainy and gray. Felix observed the yellow-painted crests of the wagons and the station clock in front of him with jealousy, how the scene was caught just as the clouds broke during a brisk winter morning. He pressed his palms into his face and leaned back on the glass window. In the third carriage, snug on a red-painted couch, sat a poodle, wagging his mechanical tail.

Boon had disappeared soon after the required signatures. He was more accustomed to *le grasse matinée* Monday mornings when half of the workers would be late, so had started towards a nearby park without so much as a goodbye or mention of a time he would return. While all of Paris had woken up in the same lazy way—listening to the wind hitting the windows— Boon had woken up with a kick in the ribs when Felix had run into him on the way to the bathroom. And perhaps because of this, while everyone was still rubbing the weekend out of their eyes, he was as charged as ever.

He was holding coins in his left pocket as he opened the phone booth, and picked a golden twenty centimes to begin with. He dialed the phone number quickly, recently more practiced than usual, and waited for the call to go through.

"Hey—"

What's going on? The other voice broke out in thick Thai.

Boon readjusted his earpiece. "Nothing. Why?"

We agreed not to call more than necessary.

"It's necessary." Boon said, also thinking, *it's been too long.*

Then on with it, what's the problem?

"Plans changed. We're going to take the train." He squinted at the cloudy sky.

Not flying?

"I know, but it's less risky. Less control in Moscow, I'll tell you about it later. Not here."

I understand.

There was some hesitation on the other end, something caught in a breath.

Listen, we're still—

"Yes," and Boon felt the fierceness in his own voice, "we're coming one way or another."

You have to.

"I know. We will."

He doesn't know, right?

Boon had hardly kept up pushing in coin after coin, listening to the man's voice over the metallic *zing!* of the machine. He only had a few francs left.

"No," he let out a sigh, "I won't tell him till we get there. About a week. Maybe more."

That's long.

"I know."

Just, don't slip up Boon.

"I won't." he held onto the last coin and listened to the breathing on the line until the call expired. The booth was still cold—he hadn't been inside enough for condensation to form on the glass. Swiftly as ever, he hung up the phone and stepped into the street.

During ugly weather, ugly creatures get to work. After the robberies, A-wut and Decha had moved to a dismal hotel of five stories and twenty chambres, each fitted with a bed and nothing else. They were unlucky enough to have the topmost room where the singular hatch window leaked when it rained. The bed was so small, and the space between it and the walls so narrow they couldn't help but wonder whether the bed had been purchased to fit the room, or the room built to fit the bed. But it was central and clean and allowed them to spy on Felix without being seen. They were still trying to piece together what exactly Felix and Boon had gone to France for. In their hasty escape, they had left A-wut's jacket with the receipt inside the pawn shop, and without it, couldn't make head or tail of the whole situation.

Like the best business partners, they worked best together when they worked alone. They developed a system. Decha would leave early and sit in a cafe around the whereabouts of the bank George worked at. It was three days before Decha caught sight of him, chest puffed out over his sagging belly, on his way home. Once in the right quarter, Decha hit another bar, and stayed for dinner. He had never been to France but could gather that this was more of a local spot, with horse race scores pinned on the walls and comedian night programs written in chalk underneath the menu. He waited, sitting in a corner and ordering himself a stew *s'il vous plait*. With gossip handed out along with napkins and a drink, he would get the information fast.

In the meantime, A-wut remained in the dank hotel room, also hard at work. They had contacted the Big Man periodically since the robbery, and after hearing of the passports, for the first time, he had sounded pleased. However, because the passport business was not in their line of work, he had told A-wut to send the documents to his office in Thailand, where, through his hands, they would be distributed accordingly. Having been in the business all his life, A-wut knew surprisingly little of the organization he worked for. It didn't even have a name. As he prepared pages to send over, it was the first time he realized that somewhere, among the rank of young men who led a double life like him, there were those who dealt not with people, but with their IDs.

Because his work didn't require anonymity, A-wut would leave the hotel room promptly at noon each day and treat himself to a beautiful lunch of assorted patisserie items. Returning to his room, he'd lay the delicacies out like prizes: a prune-filled egg tart that reminded him of Thai Daan Tats, a chocolate eclair, a *chausson aux pommes*—juicy and zesty, with a golden pocket of pastry scored and baked to perfection. While some French extravaganza had A-wut tired, he reveled in their bakery. With the money and papers in neat rows on the floor, and the goods arranged in front of him, the afternoon turned delectable again.

That is, until Decha burst through the door and trampled all the work his companion had done.

"Gather up your things, we need to leave," he barked. His hands worked frantically, and because they hadn't exactly made themselves at home, he was quick to shuffle the money and papers in a pile and then into his suitcase.

A-wut had stood up and was packing his things too.

"What—"

"So the man we robbed was his friend's cousin. Felix's friend."

"Yes but—" A-wut saved the prune tart just as Decha stormed heavily across the room. He placed it on the bed.

"I asked around, at the bar—nevermind that. They've left. They took the train."

While he still had questions, A-wut stuffed the last of their belongings silently into the bags. All the color had drained out of him, his jaw was set. The Big Man would not be happy.

"Where?" A-wut said, as they looked around the room, making sure they left no trace of their stay.

Decha caught his eye. "Moscow."

And with that they grabbed the bags and left, beds undone, the door open, and the pastries, still warm from the oven, untouched.

Around the time Decha and A-wut left the hotel, Boon stepped out of the compartment for a smoke. The train was sectioned in nooks, two wide benches on the bottom and two fold-down mattresses on top. Come nighttime, half the passengers would climb on the top "bunks" while the rest made a home of the bottom ones, so that, with everyone in their striped pajamas, it felt like summer camp. That is, if it weren't in the white negatives outside.

On the train, there wasn't much privacy for despair. Everything was open to the rest. Across from he and Felix had sat two hulky men, complete with matted dublyonki coats and beards to make John Knox jealous. Not five minutes after departing they had set out a bottle of vodka and a huge jar of pickles on the table, and had started playing chess. They, Boon thought with certainty as he moved through the train, would've survived Napoleon's invasion.

During his short walk, Boon let his eyes linger on the other passengers. Mostly, people were reading. Table to table, they huddled close to one another and read yesterday's newspaper, books with weak spines, crosswords. The forty hour train ride was perhaps the only time people looked over the obituaries. Then were the sleepers, faces covered with hats, knees bent up like paper dolls. A couple of mothers nursing babies looked out the window to the unwavering brightness outside. The smokers were traversing the train like him.

When he stepped into the last compartment at last, all air left him for a second. The smoke was thick and blue and warm. For the first time that day, Boon chuckled as he lit his own cigarette, taking a seat on a bench alone.

As he ran a hand over the back of his head, he tried to convince himself he and Felix had done the right thing, or at least, the only thing to be done. Reporting the mugging hadn't been an option—they had lost the receipt for the chameleon alongside the passports and the money; Aunt Vivi would have found out he'd pawned her gift for a quarter of its value, and they had no real memory of what had happened anyways. Besides, while they'd been lucky to get new passports quickly —with no questions asked about how exactly they had lost them—they would've managed to go to Thailand and back before the police got round to investigating the crime.

Boon took a long drag of his cigarette. There was a paper envelope stuffed inside a pair of socks in his bag with enough money for the rest of the tickets to Thailand, but he dismissed the thought immediately. He needed that later. It wasn't for spending. In the meantime, he and Felix would have to find another way to get more money. Together, they had only enough for the tickets to Beijing, giving them six nights to crop for more. He had suggested they sell cigarettes and other belongings on the train—taking out his lighter and another cigarette, nothing else in his pockets, he chuckled again. They would think of something.

A man to his left offered him a drink then, *vodka*, he thought, or rather felt, as it burned down his throat and lungs, *vodichka—little water*. And indeed in a tiny, little glass it was.

Chapter 10

MOSKVA YAROSLAVSKY STATION WAS A neat building. Thick-boned and industrial, it had every look of having been built under the Republic: the roof durable, built to withstand the weather; inside, large black columns you couldn't wrap your arms around, ranked and squat under tall arches. Lit in bright yellow, everything was no-nonsense, left little to the imagination and worked as it should. A-wut and Decha needed a few seconds to take it all in.

It was snowing in Moscow, a particularly cold March. They imagined climbing onto the roof of the station and looking out into the whole city. An overwhelmingly white expanse if it weren't for the Kremlin and the icy Moskva River, a blue scar across the landscape. Even from the ground, they could see the very top onion of St. Basil's cathedral, sticking up behind the bus shed, golden and bright as a beacon.

Their flight had been short compared to the train journey, which had been delayed in Minsk, forcing the two to wait out Felix's arrival in the raw elements of Russia. Initially they had marveled at the snow, taking fistfuls each, tasting it. Used to the loud colors and noises of Thailand, the padded, white silence had mystified them. But they'd spent the night in the bus shed, being kicked out of the station for loitering, curbing their anger with the fear of approaching a Russian.

Now, running awkwardly to avoid slipping on ice or plunging a foot in a muddy and icy puddle, trying to catch himself on the station's doors, A-wut couldn't have been more fed up with it all. Starved at last, he'd gone to buy breakfast from a street side vendor. Inside the station again, he slapped his frozen cheeks a couple of times, his face having started to set like drying clay, and headed toward a bench in the bright west-wing of the station where Decha sat waiting. He handed one of two paper plates to Decha.

"*Blini*. Not too sure what's in them."

The pancakes were the size of A-wut's hand and golden brown, mounted by a steaming, creamy paste and a dollop of orange roe in the center. Warm and slightly greasy, their aroma had trailed behind A-wut all the way from the kiosk outside. As the two bit into them, the first thing they'd eaten in a day, somewhere in Heaven an angel sang.

"Halibut." A-wut decided, and for a second he forgot to be miserable.

"Listen to me," Decha said between mouthfuls, "I met our contact, he came while you were out, arrived this morning from Bangkok. He's sitting on the opposite side of the station. Don't look."

Naturally, A-wut looked. A small man, head bowed to his chest, sleeping.

"Do we know him?"

"No, he didn't say much. The Big Man says we can trust him enough."

They ate a couple blini in silence. They had been on the chase for a few weeks, longer than any other assignment, and they missed Thailand, its heat, and flavors and faces. A-wut looked at the Thai man with jealousy, his dark skin pulled tight by the sun.

"Do we have a plan?" he asked.

"No. Not yet."

A-wut looked at his own spidery hands, white from the cold, and shivered. "His name?"

"San'ya." *A promise.* "Let's hope he lives up to it."

The two finished eating in silence. Decha wiped his fingers on his pants, and was about to hand his plate to A-wut, who'd started toward a trash can, when he grabbed his partner's wrist.

"What—" A-wut said, frowning.

But Decha was pointing toward the entrance of the station, where among a wave of people that had gathered at the doors, was Felix. His friend Boon stood next to him, brushing snow from his shoulders and hair, whispering something. The two boys scanned the station, blowing in their cupped hands, glancing past the column A-wut and Decha had hidden behind. Decha counted a minute on his watch before he dared to peek back, just in time to catch the young men walking from the ticket booth to sit on a bench, tickets tucked inside their coat pockets.

Although the station had been empty moments before, swarms of people had started coming into the station and heading straight to the ticket booth. All at once, they rushed, and then all together stopped.

"This line." Decha said, pulling out a cigar, an eight inch monster, and puffing so hard the foot crackled. "Damn it."

He was not wrong.

Beginning in early April, Caribous will migrate from fertile Southern lands to the North before mosquitos can get to them, resulting in one of the largest migrations on earth. With such large heads and so little hurry, they dwindle in the fields and marshlands. And it was like this that the line proceeded.

When they finally reached the ticket desk, they were left looking at a bulldog of a man, teeth sticking out and mouth turned down toward Hell. The pancakes flipped in their stomachs.

"Everything is in cyrillic." A-wut said, examining the boards, unable to make sense of them.

"English?" Decha said to the agent. He'd taken out the money already and was hoping to make the ordeal a quick one.

Rather than reply, the man emitted what sounded like a growl as he looked them up and down.

Decha blew smoke out his mouth, slowly. "You don't speak English?" he said, with as little accent as possible, more curt than before.

The man raised a hand to point at a sign next to his window, smacking his lips before speaking. Unlike Decha, he bore his accent like a birthmark. "Here, just tickets. No smoke."

A-wut stepped in front of Decha to avoid a brawl. He'd been studying the boards, and while he couldn't understand them, he was almost sure there weren't many routes to go to Thailand. Still, he and Decha didn't know enough—who was Felix working with, or for whom and to what purpose? What other stops he had planned on the way? They needed to follow his tracks exactly.

He decided to test his luck.

"Yes, we want tickets. You see that boy?" and here A-wut pointed to Felix, who was still sitting, thankfully, not too far from the booth, "We are friends. We're going to the same place. Can we have the same ticket?"

"One ticket?"

"Two tickets." A-wut raised two fingers. The man seemed to think about something. A-wut had the sudden fear he couldn't count.

"Where?"

While A-wut audibly bit down on his molars, he hadn't given up yet. He pointed again.

"With our friends. Same ticket."

The line pushed behind them. Like Caribous annoyed by mosquitos, people have little patience for hold ups, and like the animals, they pressed on.

"Two tickets, *where?*"

This time the question had a hint of a challenge. Decha stepped forward again to have a good look at the man. While he was repulsive—yellow skin, as if it had absorbed too much smoke in its time, a snarl for a mouth—he was well taken care of, nails manicured, a neat beard. His uniform was hidden under a fur coat, warm and expensive, pinned at the neck with a singular gold brooch that held the secrets of the corrupt. His eyes, red rimmed and watery, steady on their faces, held every hint of knowing the trade.

Decha took out his wallet, pulled out a generous amount of money, and slid it through the bars of the booth.

Thankfully, A-wut still had the money they had stolen in France hidden in his bag.

The man looked at the bills without moving. Decha had begun to think he wouldn't take it when the man reached over and started stacking it neatly before folding it into an invisible pocket of his coat. He moved slowly, licking his fingers while he flipped through the records pages and ran his finger down the day's sales. He printed out two tickets that passed through Beijing, held out his hand for the cheap fare, put it neatly in the register and raised an eyebrow to dismiss them.

As they moved away from the booth, A-wut almost convinced himself that he had seen the man smile, but when he turned to get a better view of his face, it looked cruel as ever.

Chapter 11

NOT HAVING ENOUGH MONEY FOR a Kupe ticket, Felix and Boon gathered their items and began boarding the Platzkart wagon. It was a busy morning, the platform so packed that the flagmen had to jump to be seen and heard over the tumultuous chugging of the engines.

Felix stood shivering, his head ducked against the snow. Russia was finally getting to him. They were traveling with a few light layers and thinner spirits. Unlike Paris, which had been as elegant and snobbish as a cigarette in the hand of a lady, Russia was proving more blunt in its welcome. The men around Felix wore felt boots called *valenki* to brace themselves for it. Whatever made up the gritty *kasha* they'd had for breakfast was the base for the matter-of-fact language and fabric of the nation.

Boarding was progressing so slowly Felix had begun to assume, not unreasonably, that the people were stuck to the ice on the platform. His feet had gone numb. As they neared the train at last, he read a translated phrase on the side of the carriage: *so cold that the birds are freezing in mid-air!* He squinted at the white unpromising sky, grabbed onto the open doors, and jumped the last step.

Two weeks after leaving New York, with a compartment as private as the first (which was to say, as open as the Great Plains of Nebraska), Boon was quick to make himself at home. He settled into his seat, dropping the angel statuette only one time, and placed two beers and a brown bag onto the table. Just a couple of vodka, beer and pickles rounds into their last train ride, they had been heavily advised to save money on the dining car. And they had taken the men's word by God. After splurging on the tickets, Boon and Felix had ventured outside of Yaroslavsky station and, finding a supermarket, had bought some provisions. Stuffed between their shirts and socks were cups and cups of flavored instant mashed potatoes, small bags of *syrniki*, a separate bag bursting with tomatoes that Felix had kept out of their luggage for safekeeping, and—of course—four jars of *solen'ya* to be eaten with every meal.

Boon opened a jar and was picking up the first pickle when the train started to move. Felix was sitting with his chin on his hands, admiring the snowing scene outside their window, when a piercing cry shot across the station. A mother had succeeded in hauling her child onto the car, but had been shut out by the closing doors. Only by a miracle, she managed to pull them open again and jump in. Nothing is as punctual as the Russian train: if it's meant to leave at eleven am, it will leave at 11:00m:00s.

As in most games of cops and robbers, there had been someone spying on Felix from the first bite of pickle to the last, and it was Decha who took the honor of starting the chase again. He had easily spotted Felix and his friend among the *ushanka* hats on the platform, the only other Thai faces. On the train, his own bench was stationed just two behind theirs, with A-wut parallel on the other side, and San'ya hidden a carriage away.

"At least," he told A-wut as they sank into the hard cushions, patting his empty wallet, "we bought good seats."

While Felix had felt his entrance on the train to be somewhat underwhelming, as most things are after a lot of travel, Decha was on edge. A package had fallen from one of their bags onto the floor, and although fleeting, he couldn't put to rest the horrified expression Felix had made before retrieving the box and stuffing it deep into his bag. Decha spent a large part of the afternoon, imagining what it could be, and, more importantly, how they could steal it.

"A weapon?" he asked, "Drugs?" He'd been staring out his window, absorbing the last of the city when he turned to find A-wut asleep in his chair.

Decha contemplated until dinner, when he and A-wut trudged toward the dining car and bought the most expensive vegetable soup they'd ever had. Whatever Felix was planning, they had to find out—possibly, he thought, watching A-wut spend yet more money on some beer and carry it to their table, before the Big Man got involved himself.

Felix set only two rules for the train ride: don't spend any money, and be on time for tea. As he and Boon soon learned, around four in the afternoon, a lady with features of a matryoshka doll would serve *chai* from a pot that seemed to not run out through the whole length of the train. Each day, they spent wandering about the compartments right up until that time, when they would head back to their sleeping benches and wait for the woman to appear.

To fill the time, at first, they tried to sell some of their possessions—shirts, hats, sunglasses, souvenirs they'd bought in Paris—in hopes of making money. The rich sable-fur class had their separate carriage at the front of the train, to avoid young men pestering them with half-worn Parisian shirts and cigarettes. There, in the Kupe, there was no need for the items they were selling, and the boys were soon dismissed with the wave of a hand. People in the rest of the train, the poorer end, kept their conscience as sharp and clean as fingernails. Even the women, holding up their shawls and whispering behind them, didn't trust the boys one bit.

The third day Boon and Felix tried to sell the statue. Decha peered over the seats as they extracted the package from their bags and slipped out of the carriage. But they didn't go as far this time. Their attempts to sell the hideous figure were quickly smothered. Much like children who try to out-scare each other, people scuttled seat to seat and braced each other about the horror to come. When, just briefly after, Felix would arrive, he would be shooed away, looking so demoralized it would touch Miseria's heart.

Only once did Boon have any luck. On the way back to his seat, he stumbled into a compartment rich in the gay laughter of women, huddled and cozy together like old hens in a coop.

He hadn't gone that long, he thought, but when he pointed quizzically at the tea service on the table, not able to *ask* them the time, they instead took it as an invitation to pull him in their gossip. He ate currant bread with pears and listened to their broken English, talk of love stories and griefs they couldn't iron out with time.

Other nights, he slipped out of his bed and walked across the train with his head in his hands. He would watch the northern hills slip by and far into the dark, and he'd think to call, forgetting there were no phones he knew of in the train. It *had* been too long.

Sometimes, on nights when the stars shone brighter, one of the women would come along and hand him a woolen sweater, leaning forward for him to light her cigarette. She'd invite him and his *drook*, his friend, for tea the next day, promising another trade. Those women carried the desolation of the Steppe, the mysteries of Taiga, the inscrutable soul of Big Mother Russia. Boon would readily accept. Those nights, blue smoke twisting into itself, Felix slept with one eye open.

In the meantime, A-wut and Decha worried. Felix and his companion, Boon, would disappear morning till late afternoon, going and returning with various bags. It was obvious that they had a contact on the train, but who it was exactly Decha didn't know and couldn't easily find out himself. The constraints of traveling by train precluded any sort of close-range spying; he was limited to their carriage, which Felix and Boon would leave as promptly as dawn. When, soon after their departure, Decha had finally found sun-charred San-ya buried deep in the intestines of the train, he had instructed him to keep watch. But even San-ya, shrewd and patient as a vulture, had only ever seen Felix and Boon alone—their contact must have been further up ahead and out of sight. A-wut and Decha started to wonder if Felix and Boon were not, as they thought, just two amateurs, but actual spies—smart ones.

However frustrating, Felix's sneaking about gave A-wut and Decha time to search his things. Apart from a couple of stale bread rolls and clothes, their bags contained a book of crosswords, cuttings of old newspapers, *Thieves Steal Car, Police on the Chase!*, and a number of cigarette packs. No passports. No papers. Those Boon had been carrying around his person since they had gotten them anew. Even A-wut, checking the lining of the bags couldn't find anything worth telling the Big Man.

By the fourth day, Decha was spent. Wanting to stretch out the money they had, they had been living on rations of pâté and crackers from the dining car that cost a fortune and then some more. They didn't dare steal from Felix. After so much work they wouldn't allow themselves to be caught red-handed, especially for a stale bread roll. And so they waited, and Decha grew ever restless. He could find no apparent motives for Felix wanting to meet the Big Man. Boon and Felix talked little and wrote nothing, save for some crosswords they filled abominably. Nothing that would suggest anything besides two ordinary young guys from New York, nothing that would satiate a stranger's curiosity. The plan, Decha finally decided, must have been in their minds alone. Here, possibly, were the most cunning professionals they had come across for a long time.

By the last day on the train, the thieves were getting desperate. Unbeknownst to them, so were Felix and Boon—Beijing sounded like a harsh city to set foot in without money. The train had passed various arid paintings of the countryside, where poverty blazed like an ugly tear in silk. So when A-wut approached the two friends with a small bow, and offered them a deal, little did he know that it was the best prospect for getting money that Felix and Boon had had the whole trip.

"You said poker, right?"

"Yes, poker, *pok deng*." A-wut repeated. The three had jumped over formalities and were speaking in rapid Thai. "There's a man in the next train car that would like to play with you. You see, he's an avid player, and I've been playing with him all week. He's a dear friend. But, frankly, I've lost a considerable amount. I'm no good with cards, I see right through them."

A-wut had rehearsed the whole thing and was laying it down perfectly. Decha was watching from his seat and San-ya was waiting at his own table with the cards in hand.

The language undulated between them. There was something so soothing about it. Or maybe, Felix thought, it distracted from the barren snow outside. Felix and Boon didn't have to talk for long. They didn't have enough rubles to get them anywhere and had just enough to play. The choice, really, came down to the time.

They agreed to go soon after the chai service.

As they soon learnt after shaking hands and sitting opposite him, San-ya was equal parts clever and impenitent. He would play a card and play it fully. When he bet, he did so carefully, with eyes narrowed and bouncing all over, checking the table as if it might suddenly switch. San-ya wore his features without pride but without embarrassment either. When he gave an ugly snarl you knew that he meant to. He was quick handed and a little frantic in the shuffling. It was obvious he was a master of the game.

He won the first three hands, but they'd been betting low and watching him, and on the fourth Boon cleared the table. They were learning their opponent. Well, Felix was content folding each game. He would start strong, create commotion, distract a little, and ultimately settle down with his bad hands, sighing tiredly at each loss.

Boon, however, didn't take his eyes off the man.

It was Boon's turn to shuffle, and he picked the cards up slowly. More controlled than San'ya, he riffled them evenly and bridged, little flutters like the wings of a hummingbird. He did this several times, the motion hypnotizing. Even San'ya was leaning forward with his hands spread on the table. Boon let San'ya cut the deck, then he dealt swiftly and they bet with the same purposeful silence. The stakes rose, they bluffed and suspected each other. The chai grew cold in their cups.

Fundamentally, Boon didn't trust San'ya. A-wut had been convincingly helpful and forgettable for being among the few foreigners on the train, as had Decha. But San'ya had a darkness to him. Boon could feel it hiding behind the hoods of his eyes. A wrinkle had broken across his forehead the first time he had lost, deep and uneven. It didn't sit right with either of the two friends.

Then, San'ya fumbled and Boon won again.

Because the betting had gotten higher, and San'ya had gained too much confidence, Felix and Boon had won a good amount of money—not enough to get to Thailand but a sum that'd get them far enough. Further, definitely, than the Beijing station. When Boon won a third time, he finally set the cards down, not wanting to blow it all away.

But San'ya had watched them for six days and had been ready for them to quit.

"You can't leave when the game starts getting exciting. I'll tell you what, I'll double it, or we shake hands?"

Boon had gotten up, and paused mid-stretch. Felix didn't say anything either, looking blankly at San'ya draining his cup. The man smiled and placed both hands behind his neck.

"Gentlemen, you should at least give me the chance to even the score. You've had luck so far," San'ya said, gesturing to the money in Boon's hand with a sly nod, "and you seem to have the guts too."

Boon was thinking that luck was a capricious thing, not to be abused or counted on. And as far as his guts went, they were dropping fast toward disaster. But right when he was opening his mouth to decline the offer, he noticed a most mocking glint in San'ya's eyes.

"Sure. One more game, you got it."

Felix raised his eyebrows and stole a worried glance at his friend, but he sat back down for the game.

"I reckon I've lost about a thousand US dollars so far. You must be short of two thousand there." He pulled out an envelope and started flicking through the bills. "To spare time counting, I'll match you," he continued, and put twenty hundred dollar notes on the table. He coughed to stop himself from smirking.

But as he started to shuffle, Boon could tell he was nervous. They picked up their cards in silence. Boon had two kings and two tens. Though good at bluffing, San'ya had nothing. He was also only a card short from a straight. They both exchanged one card. Boon got a queen—bad luck. San'ya got a nine. They nodded before putting the cards on the table.

"Huh," San'ya said, flicking a piece of fluff that had floated on his cards, "you win again."

Boon's mouth was hanging open as he examined the cards again, but Felix, weary of the man, picked up the money and put it in his pocket before slapping his friend's back, grinning. Still stupefied, Boon extended a hand to shake goodbye, but realized, with a groan, that the man wasn't going to be easy to shake off. He almost looked offended by Boon's hand.

"I hear you have an antique with you, gentlemen?"

The question was layered with his darkness and something beyond an honest interest to play poker. Boon and Felix looked at each other and found there was only one thing they could say.

After a pause, Felix replied. "Yes, do you collect?"

"I do. That's my job. I'm currently on my way to an antique store in Beijing. I heard you had a knickknack here yourself." He scratched a thought from his left ear. "And will you be staying in Beijing as well?"

"No, we're going to Thailand, through the Mongolian line," continued Felix. Perhaps because he'd been taught to trust no one in New York, he'd grown up trusting just about everyone else instead.

"Ah." San'ya said, clicking his tongue a couple of times. "On business?"

"Visiting family, my father."

A likely story, San'ya thought, but he dismissed that thought quickly lest they saw it in his eyes. He wasn't going to get anything from them, they weren't as high-level as Decha feared, but just as shrewd. So he switched tactics instead.

"Lovely. So what do you say you play one last game for the antique? You put that down, and I bet the equivalent."

The question hung in the air with the same impatience as the man. When he saw them hesitate he wrote a figure in the thousands on a napkin.

It was Felix who came to his senses first and agreed. There was no risk of losing money. They had tried to get rid of the angel statue for six days on the train, and people had not wanted it even for free. Seeing it had chilled even the most solemn Russian to the bone. And here was a man willing to bet for it blind. If Felix didn't rush away to fetch it while Boon shuffled the cards, he did the next thing to it.

Unfortunately for San'ya, he had mistaken their eagerness for agitation, and felt even surer that whatever the antique was, it would lead them all closer to discovering the boy's business in Thailand. The game was very easy. Boon placed the wrapped statue in the center. He looked at his cards, got a full house, and folded.

"Good game," Boon said with false disappointment. He couldn't believe they had gotten rid of the eyesore at last, and he felt relieved to see the glint back in the man's eyes. Somehow, the man had been more unsettling without it.

San'ya straightened his back as he finally shook their hands and let them go, his smile the most genuine since they'd joined him for the game. Luck, indeed, is a capricious thing.

They had played longer than expected, and by this point, the train had begun rolling slower and slower into the city of Beijing, passing apartments with windows open and laundry drying on the balcony racks. Before the train had stopped on the platform, Boon and Felix were standing ready at the doors with their belongings, absorbing the aromas from outside and possibility around them.

San'ya was left to do the opposite. As soon as they had left his compartment he had snatched the package and unwrapped it. His breath had caught. Between tulle paper and neat yarn bows, it stood in front of him, ugly as a nightmare. While people started pushing past him off the train, he waited for A-wut and Decha to retrieve him. It was too late to go after Felix and his friend. So San'ya sat there, confused, angry and downright upset, because he was sure he had played a good amount of money, four thousand dollars exactly, for the Devil itself.

Chapter 12

WHEN THEY STEPPED OUT INTO humid Beijing, Decha's face was blacker than ever, and bore a path through the sea of Chinese faces waiting to board the next train. They caught sight of Felix climbing onto a train set for Vietnam, but didn't make a move to follow.

At first, on a direct train to Phuket, A-wut and Decha tried to decipher the meaning of the statue. Despite how ugly the ornament was, or perhaps because of it, they were convinced there must have been a second meaning behind it. However, their scheming ended promptly when A-wut sat in front of a kicking child for thirty-seven hours, leaving Decha to mutter their plans to himself.

It was hard to tell who was having a worse time: Decha, who flinched each time A-wut swore; the child, who got terribly uneasy with all the muttering; A-wut, who sat in the middle of it all; or the other passengers, who had to silently endure the whole thing. It was stuff that made men go crazy. Once in Thailand, their teeth ground to stubs, they had no regards to give. They went straight to the Big Man, handed him the chameleon, the paperwork, the statue and a brief account, before retiring, finally, at home, with no intention to leave it for a week.

Conversely, the rest of the journey was quite uneventful for Felix and Boon. There were a couple more stops before reaching Thailand—Hanoi and Ho Chi Ming in Vietnam, then Siem Reap in Cambodia. They slept all day and all night. They ate seldom and voraciously, waking for tea service and an egg-filled rice ball snack.

Felix and Boon arrived in Thailand in an unglamorous manner. From Cambodia, their only option, the private tour bus, had been a nine hour hellish investment that robbed them of their money and spirits. The road they traveled on had been filled with potholes, the passengers uncommonly rowdy, and everything smelled of sweat and goats no matter how many windows were opened. The bus stopped too often and they slept terribly. It was a comparable nine hours to A-wut's thirty-seven—they would have nightmares of the bus and then wake up in it. Two hours from the arrival, Boon even lost his last pack of Newports: after a woman asked him for a smoke, he handed her the whole packet, his travel lighter, wished her a dreamy goodnight, and fell asleep.

But Phuket was alive with a hot sun that made the colors brighter and gave an edge to the shadows on the underside of leaves. They could hear the loud hubbub of the station before stepping off the bus, accompanied by the wet wind blowing in through the opened windows. The bus had rolled under a pavilion for shade, and with the rare efficiency of men who had to work in the hot underbody storage, their bags were already lined on a short concrete wall when they stepped off. It was a bit of a walk to the station entrance, and Felix was sweating under his backpack. He could feel his clothes pressing against his shoulders in bulky shapes.

It wasn't that big of a place, but they reached the entrance in a sort of stupor. Perhaps it was the wind pulling on their ears, or their packs catching on the people pushing past them, or simply because they were weary with sleep and hunger and travel. As they reached the swinging doors, stepping into the slightly cooler ticket hall, Felix sighed with the relief of someone who'd been living on the road. At least, he thought, they now had nowhere they *needed* to go.

Unlike in Moscow, the ticket booths were plentiful and decorated in meticulous red detailing, which shone brilliantly in the morning light. Through the windows opposite the bus parking lot, they could see white chrysanthemums and damask rose bushes, near them a bael tree with some heavy fruits rotting at its base. It seemed that, outside the station, everything was quiet under the balmy wind.

But they hadn't marveled at the country long when, again, they were surrounded. While both Felix and Boon had all the looks of being Thai and even spoke the language, something about their lighter skin, their American bags or, most importantly, their uncertain glances about the place, had alerted every taxi and tour guide in the vicinity and had propelled them to clamor at the boys. The station was far from empty. In fact, Boon had been watching a young girl argue with some policemen not too far away. It was an odd scene, and it had caught his attention. She, in sandals, with a furious look about her, as if she'd stood outside too long and was holding the wind in her fists. In front of her, Khaki brown guards—complete with shiny buttons and crooked teeth.

The policemen, jostled by the growing crowd, now turned toward Boon instead. The very moment the two friends had stepped onto the bus, they had felt the no-nonsense attitude of Thailand. From the five hand fans tied to the grab poles with strings whirring fiercely at the heat, to the dusty spare tire they'd had to change halfway through their journey, it was obvious that, here, a job needed doing was a job done. So with fewer words than badges on their shirts, the policemen parted the commotion and led the boys outside, pulling the girl by her elbow close behind.

Felix had expected her to pull away from the officers, or talk back, or at least prowl away into the crowd. But she stood there in the warmth and blossom of late March with her toes set apart and her black hair falling from a loose pin. While the rest of them seemed to wear the sun like a heavy skin, everything about her glowed. She turned to them before they had a chance to look away.

"Where are you going?" she asked.

Felix had been anxious about where they would stay in Phuket. They didn't have enough money for a hotel now that they'd spent so much on the bus tickets, and he was worried about staying in a beach shack, something Selena had warned him against. He had half-heartedly suggested that they could stay with his real family, once they would meet, but Boon had not been in a discursive mood, what with a fan blowing down his neck and a baby crying behind him, and had looked back sadly, closed his eyes, and the topic had not been approached again.

"Phuket." Felix said finally.

She cracked a smile. "Well, you seem to have made it."

"Yeah, I guess so. I never imagined I'd see this station."

"You have an accent." she said, stepping closer to them.

Felix was fluent in Thai and kept it up regularly by speaking to Boon, but he wasn't surprised. "New York will do that to you."

"New York! That's a long journey. You flew in an airplane all the way here? There is an airport in Phuket but I've never met anyone who has actually flown."

"We come from Paris, actually." Boon added, grabbing her hand and kissing it.

Felix rolled his eyes at Boon, who'd smirked when, simultaneously, she smiled and cocked her head, a wrinkle appearing on her forehead. He looked around for street signs indicating the way to the old town center. The sweet hours of the morning had quickly given way to the afternoon, and he was starving.

The girl was very observant. In fact, while they'd been talking, Felix had had the feeling that he was being examined—not with judgment exactly, but the way a museum curator might look at an artifact. She picked up on his distraction.

"If you're hungry I can show you my favorite place to eat. It's right on Sea Gypsy Island. If we go quickly, we'll avoid the traffic."

And, again, just as Felix was about to ask, she beat him to it.

"I'm Dara, by the way."

They set off through a couple of deserted roads, then cut across some wild lawns and bushes of hibiscus where a thin path would be hatched out messily among the flowers.

In late March, the grasses grew thick over Thailand's red soil, covering the land in dark green, spilling into the dirt roads and creeping over the hills, holding fast to the altitude with tiny little fists. It was soft beneath their feet. They were walking under Flame of the Forest trees adorned with their brilliantly orange bloom; under the boughs of rose apple trees that, come June, would bend into the road from the weight of the magenta fruit. From Spring well into Fall, one walking through Phuket would smell the citrusy sweetness of flowering plants, and nothing from the dead odor of the sea to the aromatic night markets could overcome it. The land swelled in healthy vegetation, the wilderness and weeds feeding off heavy water and thriving in neglect.

Along the road they'd taken, they had encountered only a couple of houses—flat, cheap structures so unique to themselves and the disorganized arrangement of flower pots on their porches assured that each could be told apart at night. And yet, before either of the boys could prepare for it, they stumbled off the path into an alleyway of shanties so tightly packed they formed one impassable wall.

"This way!" Dara called, moving expertly around people gathered at the trailers and huts.

This wasn't the traffic she'd been talking of, but one she seemed careful to avoid. They advanced swiftly, overhearing stories about husbands and old age, told with a furtiveness born out of the dusty outskirts of a town. The structures became more and more orderly as the three moved away from the bus station and toward the sea. To avoid the tides, the houses rose up on bamboo stilts, wooden paneling with nipa palm roofs that kept the shade cool and the monsoon rains out. Felix was about to stop to look at them when Dara turned off the road and entered one that stuck out over the edge of the water. *Brunch Out,* Felix read on the door, as they made their way in.

The bar would've held half its customers had three of its walls not been rolled back, allowing the red tables and chairs to spill on a shaded porch. There was a quiet radio playing old Thai rock songs, which, with a quiet shock, Felix realized he recognized. Dara straddled a bar stool and sat down, followed by the two boys. She ordered them pineapple slushies and basil and steak sandwiches, which they readily paid for, ate, and ordered again. People started trickling in as they finished their drinks. It was beautiful so close to the water. Felix marveled at the sea and the crabbing baskets hung above their heads on strings, laughing at Dara's stories between mouthfuls of what was possibly the best sandwich he'd ever had.

Although she found Felix and his friend to be good company, and was curious to hear about their trip, Dara's interest was sparked, in part, by jealousy.

She had turned eighteen in the rainy month of August, sitting on the back steps of her house cutting Yai's hair. Every month they'd return to the stairs, Dara with her legs tucked under and Yai on a step below, watching the dark wisps tumble off into the sand beneath them.

He'd been living with her for a year now—she was glad to have found him for many reasons. First, she had always wanted a brother. Her own mother, Chala, suffered from a severe case of pneumonia the year it spread through Phuket, a rainless spring that made the grass grow brown, and died fitfully in the night. Dara had been nine, and was given three days off school to mourn. But even at a young age, she quickly found peace in knowing that Chala had at least died around the things she loved. It was very simple. Chala had died in her own bed, and if there was anything her mother loved it was her house.

Chala had been a precocious girl. She had married Dara's father young, a serious spirit who had become unhappy before he had become a man, and they'd bought a home when she had turned twenty, a two-story townhouse at the end of a residential road, where two more streets met and formed a quiet square. It was an area of town that had avoided much of the 70's tourism, and so the houses were more dignified than those on the market or the beach. Chala was an artist. She had painted it lilac, and whenever something broke it was she who hurried to get nipa rope to fix it. She welcomed no plumber or carpenter into her home. It was a place of creation.

She wasn't a warm woman, but tidy and with an eye for beauty, which could have been why she never paid much attention to Dara—who had been a scrawny child before she grew into her skin. Chala herself was an artifact, thick hair and lighter eyes than what was common, drawn to everything nice to look at, like a magpie.

She would sit cross legged in front of an easel for days on end, and shoo Dara away when she came in to see.

"You're breathing on my neck, *tee ruk*, now go see if your father needs anything."

Dara had few memories of her mother outside of the house, and fewer memories of talking with her father. Whether he needed her or not, he never once called for her.

Chala was an intense woman until she died. She had little to say to others, unless they disturbed order in the house or her art. Dinner time was quiet. Around the neighborhood and among Dara's school friends, she was known for her coldness and beauty. But perhaps, what some people considered, it was hard for Chala to completely love her daughter, for she was the one thing she couldn't dust off and touch up with latex paint. For an artist, it must have felt intimidating to produce something so unlike herself.

When she died, having been the sole person in charge of the house, the walls took on a gloom, so dark that Dara had to go to bed at seven, and do her school reading on the porch steps. Hard as she tried, adding lamps and drawing back the shades in every room, there was nothing to be done about the light.

Her father, Sunan, had practiced strict Buddhism all her life, but when Chala died, he joined a monastery and left Dara to fend for herself. Yai, at least, was someone she could live with.

Especially, however, she was glad to have saved Yai's life.

It was a serene June day. She had been sitting on her back stairs repairing a rattan ball that had come undone during the latest *Sepak Takraw* game, when Yai passed on the street. Had she not been fed up with the stiff material and entertaining herself with people watching, she wouldn't have noticed a man following the boy. It wasn't obvious, but the man was most definitely a hunter—he wouldn't move his eyes off the boy. Dara acted on instinct. She ran down the stairs and across the street, grabbing the boy's hand—hard, so he couldn't pull away —and started walking back toward her house, saying loudly how glad she was to see her brother. He was maybe six and stumbled on the dirty road as she ran ahead. For a moment she was worried that the man would follow them. But when she reached the second-floor landing and looked back, the man had already vanished, slunk away into some rotten crevice that the city was so full of.

The boy, Yai, was living in East Phuket with a woman who took in children whose parents were too poor to look after them. So when Dara suggested he live with her, in her nice two story home, the woman readily agreed.

Every afternoon, she would bring Yai with her to school and then to work, where he would play with marbles as she prepped vegetables and cleaned the kitchen of an eatery on main street. It was owned by a tiny woman by the name of Khun Ao, widowed at thirty and never remarried. She helped raise Dara with a strict hand in manners and hot food. After learning that her mother died, she would even sew the occasional skirt.

The eatery was popular. Her specialty, Khao Tom Mad, a sticky rice and banana pudding wrapped in banana leaf, was known all over Phuket for being the best. She was a jovial woman, sharp as a pin when it came to men and money, so that she never fell in debt with either.

When she came to know that Dara had invited Felix and Boon to stay at her house, she cooked a big feast—*Gaeng Daeng*, fried rice, steamed fish with lime, and *laab*—and left it, ever so sneakily, on the back staircase, so when Yai woke up early to check on the laundry outside, he found the food still warm.

Chapter 13

IT WAS PERHAPS THE WILD beauty of the sunsets, or the pink and purple azaleas blushing in the parks which children stepped on tippy toes to smell while going to school, or maybe the white-throated kingfishers, bright and cerulean blue, soaring between palms and papaya trees along the beach, or the smell of Pad Thai, and the wonderful aromas of fresh custard bread and mango sticky rice, or that one point during the night when the gibbons would start to call to one another across the city, or a combination of these things, but Felix had fallen in love.

He hadn't many memories of Thailand, yet as they explored Phuket, certain feelings resurfaced. They had taken a *songthaew* to get to the Old Town, and while Boon had never been on one of these before—a cousin of the pickup truck with benches in the open back—the rocking and jostling were almost familiar to Felix. Walking through the streets in the evenings, when the tourists and locals came out to shop and eat and make the most out of the cooler hours of the day, a certain word or scent would catapult him to a similar moment fourteen years before.

Both boys were bewildered that Dara lived alone, but soon came to enjoy the fact and acclimated to her rhythms of life.

In the mornings the three left early, completing all the touristic must-dos Dara could think of before anyone else arrived. They went to pet elephants at a local sanctuary; they admired the intricate designs of the Hok Nguan Kung and Kiew Tien Keng shrines; with time on their hands, they even visited Koh Sirey island and its endless rubber plantations. She showed them local spots too, bringing them to her work and school and climbing on the roof of the tallest building in main street, a western-style hotel, to watch the sunset.

As he fell in love with Thailand, somewhere along the lefts and rights of the city, Felix developed a liking for Dara too. There was an ease about her and the stories she told.

"One time, and this was terrible by the way." They were sitting cross-legged on the back stair landing, Dara cutting slices of guava for everyone, Boon, Felix and Yai, before eating one herself. They would spend the hottest part of the day, the hottest afternoons, within the shade of her house, waiting to venture out again at night.

"It was July, and absolutely sweltering. I had moved to sleep in the living room, because the back of the house remains cooler at night. Yai was sleeping in the other room. I had school the next day. And I'm just about settled on the weaved sofa, trying to fall asleep again, when right next to me I hear a Tokay." She ate another slice of fruit to let the suspense broil.

"Some people say that your grandparents are reincarnated as these lizards to come look after you. But most children are scared of them, as I was. They don't look like normal geckos. They're blue and orange with rough skin, bright yellow eyes and a big mouth. Parents use them to make children behave. I think it's similar to your bogeyman."

Felix was impressed, and raised his eyebrows. She noticed and blushed a little.

"It's always in American movies. Anyway, Tokays make an odd sound, like wood creaking. A high pitched guttural noise. Terribly annoying and scary. And here there was one right next to my ear."

"Did it bite you?" Boon had gone to grab another guava, and had stopped cutting slices at her pause.

"Of course! They hate to be disturbed. Turns out I had trapped its tail underneath my shoulder and when I made the slightest move to roll away it attached itself on my upper arm. And Tokays don't let go easily either. You either wait for thunder, another superstition, or you submerge them in water, which is what I did. I filled the bathtub, all the while with this creature biting into my arm, and only after staying under for some minutes did it let go to breathe. Their teeth are tiny, thankfully."

Still, the three boys ran their fingers over the bumps on her arm with a certain fascination.

"I'm surprised you haven't heard them already. They crawl in at dusk and go off all night long."

Another time, they went to visit her father.

It was the first overcast day since their arrival, and thankfully the rain was hot and indecisive, coming on and off as they trekked their way from the songthaew drop off point to the temple. The path took them over various muddy stretches of undergrowth, but because the boys had sold any nice garments on the trains and were wearing their worst clothes already, the rain couldn't do much to worsen their appearance. The temple grounds were very clean, with the roads washed of dust and the earthy scent of Indian laurels cleansing any stench of gasoline from the road.

Thankfully, there was a break from the rains just as they reached the Viharn, the main praying hall and most important part of the temple. Not wanting to go inside wet, they waited a couple of minutes until a young monk came out and Dara, after giving a high *wai*, asked if he could find Luang Pho Sunan. He nodded and they waited some more. The temple was one of the oldest in the region, nestled some distance away from Phuket Town and closer to the hills than any other. A little way south, the monastery supported a tiger sanctuary, a large natural pond, and an elementary school. It was a known temple around the area, very active in the community and, as they would find out later, often featured in the news.

The monk returned quickly. While Dara had mentioned that she looked nothing like her parents, neither Boon nor Felix would have guessed that the man he had accompanied, so unlike their expectations, was her father. They gave deep wais to hide their shock.

Luang Pho Sunan had never been an imposing man, but now his shoulder blades stuck up and his scalp was pulled taunt, his cheeks sunken in while the skin on his neck and down his arms hung loose around the bone. Felix guessed that, at seven years old, Yai weighed more than him. The monk's voice had turned quiet over the years, whether out of solitude or lack of substance to give it strength, and after greeting them politely, he suggested they take a stroll through the grounds with the same uncertainty of the weather.

The Wat complex was bigger than they had thought. Walking slowly past each building, Luang Pho Sunan would recall its name and function and whisper it to them.

"My favorite place," he said, as they came onto an outside gazebo fitted with a small Buddha statue and an offerings table, all adorned with water jasmine vines and golden details.

They moved on. He showed them the Bot hall where he was ordained and the eight Sima stones surrounding it, the Ho Trai, stilted over a small pond which historically helped keep insects away from the holy scriptures.

"The Chofah and Naga statues, both symbolic in Buddhism," he said when they came to the crematorium, with its endless chimney and breathtaking wedding-cake roof.

There was no talk of Dara, her school, or her life. In fact, he most often addressed Boon and Felix instead, with no curiosity about their own lives. When, having reached the Vihran once more, Luang Pho Sunan smiled, and walked away from the three of them, bobbing his head above his enormous Kasaya without saying a word. It occurred to Felix, then, that the man had had no interest to talk to them at all.

Back at the entrance, they bowed deeply to the guarding Chinthe lion-like statues, and walked hurriedly away. It had started raining again. Once back on the main road, they stopped at a dessert shop and ordered banana pancakes, waiting for the sky to clear up again. Dara had been less talkative than usual. The three of them were sitting under the veranda of the store with the heavy gushing of the water on the pavement—there was little to distract from the silence between them. They ate grass jelly milk tea to cool off the heat. Felix could feel the dampness of the air sticking to the back of his knees and neck and ordered a glass of ice to go along with the drink.

"Ice," Dara said, raising her eyebrows, "how American." But the food had had a good effect on her, for she was smiling. Without much pestering, she explained about their visit at the monastery.

"It's a strict community that's very involved in politics. Currently, the monks are holding a hunger strike against the appointment of the newest local governor."

"Now, while Buddhism has called for fasting historically, this temple is one of the oldest, most populous in the district, and has a lot of influence on others. They suspected there was unfair play in the election, and have been sustaining a hunger strike for months. This wouldn't be a problem or attract too much attention, if so many people hadn't died for it already. It doesn't look good for the government."

"It's a peaceful thing really," she explained, "but if half the monks in the most important monastery of the region were to die, the consequences wouldn't be well received nationally."

They ordered some fried banana fritters that no one was hungry enough to eat, and continued listening to the dark rumbling around them. Suddenly, however, Dara chuckled.

"It seems like we've exhausted all the things to do here."

Both Felix and Boon grinned. But really, besides the strange visit, Felix was elated. The week had gone brilliantly. Just that morning he had managed to locate the address he had come here to find. Each day, he'd gone to the library, consulting maps, and asking the almost-blind librarian to help him translate the symbols and find means of transportation.

Tomorrow, he would go to see his family, and he was thrilled. But with the clouds pressing down on them, he simply smiled again.

"What a shame," he said as he scooped another jelly cube into his mouth, "I was just starting to have fun."

Felix had decided to take a motorcycle taxi to reach the house and, holding tightly onto the flabby stomach of the driver in front of him, he was regretting his decision. His face was too close to the man's slick hair, which smelt strongly of cigarettes and a pine-scented aftershave.

"And you're sure this is the right way?" Felix shouted into his ear.

"Yuh." Or such as the equivalent reply in Thai.

They had traveled quickly through the city, past banana trees and oleanders heavy with the previous day's rains, onto a narrow road that wound between a wilder foliage that gave no sign of thinning out. The sun was high in the sky, as it had been most lunchtimes, but the road didn't seem bright enough, as if the blackish leaves were capturing the light and hiding it.

Felix felt sick. Between the man's acrid shirt and the hot smell of cement, he was ready to get off by the time they turned out of the treeline and onto a reservoir. Because they'd been speeding, his face was whiplashed by the wind. Even in the open, though the sun hit his neck with heat, the day remained gloomy. It was a cheerless sun, the sticky kind that reached its tendrils down and covered everything in a sweaty film. Before he could take a final look at the lake, they plunged into the jungle again.

The motorcycle came to a stop at the end of a driveway that, by twisting behind some trees, kept the house hidden from sight. He paid the driver, who grunted in thanks and left off before Felix could turn around and see him go. A thick slab of sandstone marked the property, and engraved, the address matched the slip of paper Felix had shown to the driver before they'd set off. Here was where his family lived.

It was still a long way to the property, and he was out of breath by the time he reached the house front. It was unlike anything he'd yet seen in Phuket. While, in the city, the houses were generally modest things, and those that lined the forests suffered from leaky patchworks of corrugated metal roofs, this house gave every hint of being expensive.

Felix could tell it was designed with Western influence. Stone arches shaded a first floor porch, decorated with wicker rocking chairs and ottoman tables. Behind those were floor to ceiling glass-paneled doors, pulled back to let the air circulate inside. The tiled roof and cream walls complemented the cherry wood trimmings, and when the golden shower trees would bloom, as they had begun doing, the whole house was lit in an incredibly bright yellow hue. Later at night, the wooden shutters would be pinned back onto the wall, but to keep the rooms cooler during the day they were fastened shut over the windows, so that when Felix arrived he could see a carved-out heart right in the center of each one.

The door was open, giving onto a great hall floored in white marble, onto which shadows jumped and catapulted and colors grew brilliant. There was a breeziness about the place that surprised him, a wind that made the lace curtains billow and twist and come alive. The house looked empty, but filled with a restlessness and potential that got him ringing the doorbell before he realized he had done it.

Almost immediately a man came from the garden, seeming to chew the inside of his left cheek. He was wearing loose overalls and good boots, and was carrying a dirty shovel.

"Are you looking for Shyuri?" he asked, seeming to startle himself but looking carefully at Felix, as if to catch the same reaction in the boy.

Felix hesitated. He had never been direct, not like Boon, and didn't want to embarass himself or the gardener, but he decided to plow along anyway.

"Yes, I think, I'm his son."

The little man's eyes widened and he gave another shifty glance at Felix, then seemed relieved when he excused himself and went to fetch Shyuri from the back. It was obvious he wasn't used to giving orders, so he left Felix on the threshold. Not having been invited inside, Felix decided to wait a little way outside the house, sitting in one of the chairs scattered on the porch.

As the time passed, his hands began to shake. He had imagined many ways of meeting his family, and nothing from the long driveway, to the big house, to the rich smell of the place brought afloat any memories. For a moment he had wondered whether the gardener had been his father, or his uncle, and this scared him. What if he wouldn't recognize his family?

He had read, in a magazine in Dara's restaurant, that carrying a lucky charm into a new place was sure to keep you safe. He didn't have anything on him he could consider lucky, so he picked up the husk of an unripe tropical almond by his feet and held the green oval between two fingers. Now, he was confident that this thing would bring him as much luck as any foliage, but he tucked it in his pocket nonetheless. After all, this human uncertainty is the same that makes New Yorkers avoid stepping under ladders and throw pepper over one's shoulder after spilling salt, which more often than not gets them into trouble with whomever's eyes the pepper lands in. But, lucky or not, he needed some old fashioned superstition—what if he had gone to the wrong house? Or worse still, *what if he'd gotten it right?*

The Big Man approached with suspicion. He was fit for his name, and if you were to imagine a mountain range trying to fit through a doorway elegantly, you might imagine how the Big Man moved about. But there was something subtly controlled about him. He wore a lion's tooth proudly around his thick neck and bore the importance of the animal it was made from.

Felix was too shocked to say anything. Despite the heat, little cool whispers of air had wrapped around his ankles and made his spine go cold.

"Hello." The Big Man finally said.

He was confused at the boy's hesitation. He had received the passports and reports from A-wut and Decha's on their stop in Paris and then the train from Moscow. Irritably, the two goons still hadn't figured out exactly what the boy and his companion wanted from him. He had the boy's fax folded in his pocket, one of the most intricate threats or business collaboration notes he had ever received. Posing to be his son was creative, but he hadn't been able to figure out the code within, so he couldn't fully appreciate its ingenuity. He saw brilliance eye to eye. But only when he benefitted. Again he remembered he knew nothing of the boy, and this annoyed him. He grunted when Felix didn't reply.

Embarrassed, Felix gave a wai. "Hello."

The Big Man arched his eyebrows. No one in the profession bowed to anyone. "What do you want?"

Felix thought for a moment. The man was impenetrable. He looked angry and calm at the same time and, evidently, had no tolerance for chit-chat. Felix got right to it.

"Did you receive my fax?"

"Yes."

"Alright."

Now, it was Felix who was confused. The man had been ready, and yet here he was, cool and composed as ever. Maybe, he reasoned, they were talking of the wrong fax.

"From New York, I mean." Felix continued.

"Yes."

"The kid."

"Yes."

There was no emotion in the man's answers. In fact, he had begun to tilt his head backward with humor, or as if to challenge Felix, it was hard to tell. Regardless, Felix realized that he must have gotten the house wrong. This man had no interest in him, understandably, because he wasn't his family.

"Oh." Felix said, "I'm sorry to bother you, I'll show myself out."

The Big Man scrunched his eyebrows. He even gave his head a shake, like a great, dumb mastiff.

"What is it you want? Money?"

"Money?" Felix had started to go and stopped just next to a jasmine tree, its smell sweet and pungent. "No. I apologize, I got the wrong address."

Both men regarded each other silently, both confused, both unsure of what the other's intention was. The Big Man was sharper in these things, however, and he tested the possibility that this kid, this wide-eyed boy, might've actually been telling the truth.

"You said you were my son?"

"Yes."

"Why?" If he avoided the question, the Big Man thought, he would've known it was a bluff.

But Felix replied truthfully. He told the man the whole story, and even showed him the little address tag had been carrying around since he was five. It was the first time he'd ever told it in full without any emotion, for he was certain, by this point, that the address had meant nothing.

But to the Big Man, it helped lay it out clearly for the first time. Although Felix didn't notice it, there was a subtle change in the Big Man's demeanor. He both relaxed and worked himself up to a state. The kid meant no business, he wasn't a spy. But he was one of his children, one A-wut and Decha had evidently lost track of. This called for a meeting with the group; there had been talk about tagging before and he wanted to approach the subject again. But for now, the Big Man let himself find the humor in it all.

"Oh." He said, pondering every possibility of how one might do this until the boy shifted uncertainly in his spot, "Yes, I think you are my son."

In the kitchen, Felix readily accepted a cup of tea and ran his tongue along the back of his teeth. He tried to make himself believe the man.

"My name is Shyuri, and I gather that you're Felix?"

"Yes."

The two sipped in silence.

"And how old are you, Felix?"

"Nineteen."

Nineteen! And here the Big Man had been worried of a threat. He smiled pleasantly.

"Care to see the house?"

Lost in his thoughts, Felix simply nodded.

They set off across the grounds. First outside, where Chinese hibiscus and Madagascar periwinkle lined the border of the property; then, they saw red frangipani, which were similar to lei and Champa flowers but a dark crimson color; the orange jasmine bush, not to be confused with the Mexican petunias, yellow trumpetbush and Chinese violets that were on the completely opposite side of the house and, the Big Man noted, didn't get as much attention as they should.

Then, the Big Man brought Felix inside through the dining room, with floor seating influenced by traditional Thai designs. The Big Man even showed Felix his study, which was much less lavish than the rest of the house. As the Big Man went over to his desk and grabbed a cigar, pointing to the coconut trees through the french windows, he chucked to himself. Little did Felix know that his passport, among many other real and fake ones, lay just in the filing cabinets behind him.

While Shyuri was having fun giving him a tour of the house, Felix was quiet. The man was quite obviously not his father, but Felix didn't know why he pretended to be. He couldn't make sense of it. So he remained suspicious and observant, and was rewarded for both.

In talking about the style of the house, the man brought him to the library, in which he busied himself pulling architecture books off the shelves and tossing them carelessly onto an ottoman. As Felix was flipping through one, an object caught his eye. Capturing the dimming afternoon light and breaking it into a thousand green shards, so that the garden seemed to spill inside the house, the emerald chameleon stood poised on one of the shelves. With many Thai stone craftsmen, it could have surely been another, had it not been for the outstretched hand detailed in golden wire. It was the one Felix and Boon had exchanged in France for money.

Felix went through the rest of the rooms in a daze. When he excused himself to the bathroom, slapping cold water on his cheeks, he almost didn't look in the mirror. There, what could've definitely not been mistaken, or replicated, or forgotten in a life or even two, positioned almost ironically above a cat's litter box, was the ugly angel statuette that they had rather craftily disposed of in poker.

Back at the entrance, the air smelled distinctly foul. The tea churned in Felix's stomach and the cigar stench clung hungrily to them both. The air too was getting stale, ready to be stirred by night critters—bats and flying lemurs rustling between the palm and rubber tree canopy.

"We even get jungle cats." Shyrui said as Felix stepped off the porch.

"And Tokays?"

Shyuri smiled, unsettlingly so. "Yes, those too. Be careful out there."

"Will be."

"Mind the jasmine tree next to you. It's the biggest in the region, there's no plant like it."

"Who says?" Felix said, starting to walk into the night.

"My gardener," Shyuri replied, narrowing his eyes, "he's the best in Phuket too."

With everything designed to draw attention to the Big Man's power—his fertile soil, the strong European pillars—he just couldn't help getting the last word in.

Chapter 14

IN THE MEANTIME, DARA HAD just begun to wring out the laundry from the bathtub, the washing machine having stopped working during the last monsoon season, when the phone at the end of the hall rang. Her family had gotten a landline much sooner than most people in Phuket, mostly because her mother had stayed at home so much, and would listen to her friends recount gossip and local news from her balcony. Usually, the phone would ring only when Khun Suwannarat alerted Chala that the lychees were back in season at the market, which was one of the few times she left the house.

Even when phones became more common, after her mother died, Dara received very few calls. Her father had always shied away from such technology. She didn't think he'd ever used one in his life. But she awaited calls eagerly, fascinated by the idea of speaking into the receiver and twirling the cord like they did in the movies.

So without much hesitation, she threw the freshly cleaned sheets back in the water and picked up the phone.

"Sawasdee kha!"

She had spoken in Thai, naturally. It would either be Khun Ao calling for help at the restaurant, or one of her schoolmate's moms checking in on her as they occasionally would do—who else would be calling? On the other end the caller stammered a little.

"Sawasdee kha?" she repeated.

"Sawasdee kha…คุณพูดภาษาอังกฤษได้ไหม?"

The voice that replied was male and uncertain, testing the syllables the way one might try a new food. Static rippled across the line. The sounds were thicker than usual, the voice accented, and with a shock Dara realized it was an international call. *This* was something else entirely. She had to sit down.

It took a moment for her to process. Someone outside of her small life was calling her. She held the receiver in both hands and looked out the window. She was a *phone number*, and it was exhilarating. Dara was so shocked that she almost missed the question, *do you speak English?*

"No, I'm sorry." For a moment Dara wondered if the man would hang up.

"Well, I'll try my best then, I'm not very fast in Thai." He stopped speaking again, as if to warm up his mouth for the words to come. "Is this the residence where I can find Boon Mee?"

"Yes?"

"Good. And whom am I speaking to?"

Dara had answered without hesitation, giddy from the surprise, but something about the man's tone made her think twice about the question. He sounded scared.

"His landlady." she said, "I can pass on a message."

The man thought about it. Dara tapped her fingers on the receiver.

"Will Boon be back shortly?"

"I doubt it." In fact, she had no idea where he had gone.

"Ah, well, if you could take a message then."

While he'd spoken with an accent, something fluid and European, he had managed to keep up with her. Now, he took a long time to choose his words.

"Tell him that I took the money, and the passports. But I don't have them now." Something brushed against his receiver and he cleared his throat. "Two men stole it from me. Say 'Goaty I'm sorry' just like that."

Money. Passports. Stole. She held her breath until she realized that the message was over. She was listening to his breathing just as he was to hers. And again, the cracking of the line made her anxious.

"It will get to him." And as much as she'd enjoyed the call to begin with, she couldn't wait to get off. In fact, she felt as if her house had been intruded in.

The man seemed to have thought the same, because he gave a quick thanks and hung up. As soon as she heard the line go down, Dara cursed at herself. Distracted by the accent and the message, she had forgotten to ask for a name.

When Felix arrived from a walk not soon after, bringing a paper bag of fried squid from a nearby food kiosk, Dara was still uneasy from the call. After folding the laundry, she'd sat on the floor in front of the couch with her head on her knees, biting her nails, thinking, and had come to no conclusion. Felix also seemed shaken, talking little and regarding the orchid vase or something behind it with a frown. As they ate the squid and sipped sweet oolong tea, he came to sit next to her, both stealing glances at each other over the brim of their cups.

"Someone called today." Dara finally said.

"Is that what's bothering you?"

Dara blushed behind her cup. In two weeks, she felt that Felix knew her better than anyone yet. With good memory, she replayed the conversation almost verbatim, describing everything from the tone to the lulls in the accent. The two boys had recounted parts of their journey to her—teatime on the Moscow train, the bus journey into Phuket—but nothing about their disastrous time in Paris. The chameleon and the money were matters left to themselves alone. But now Felix told her vaguely about the mugging, and while Dara's face scrunched up with confusion thinking about it, an idea came to Felix.

"What if Boon hired someone to pretend to steal from us? And now, even if the guy was lying about not having the money, they have to get in contact?"

Dara nodded slowly. "He even called Boon a code name, *Goaty*."

Felix was obviously not happy with his conclusion, but didn't propose any other alternatives. Instead, he frowned deeper and mumbled, "We agreed to only give this number to our families, for emergencies."

Dara nibbled on a piece of fried squid and watched a little crease appear in the middle of his forehead. When he didn't look up again, she said, "How did it go today?"

The moment she said it, his whole body slumped against her. He leaned back against the couch with his hands behind his head and let his eyes linger on her face.

"Not how I was expecting it."

"Well," Dara started. But she still couldn't tell how badly it had gone.

"Does it ever?" Felix said, finishing her thought. "The house is beautiful, everything's new and lacquered on. The garden too, it's just…splendid."

"So the address was right? You did meet your family?"

"Not exactly. Or at least, *I* didn't think so. I mean, this six-four, 300 pound man came up to me." He stood up, spun in a circle and looked Dara in the eye, "There was just *no way* we were related. But then he brought up the fax and, the way he talked about it, he was very aware of it and was trying to understand my intentions, I guess. But I could feel–I have good intuition, or that's what my mother says—and at first I thought he was humoring me before kicking me out and sending me a fine for the flowers I'd trampled while walking in." He stopped to think for a moment, picking up a pen and clicking it in and out a couple of times. "He wanted to know if I was asking for money, all suspicious like. But when I tried leaving, because, *evidently* I had gotten the wrong house—well, then he tells me I'm his son."

"And then it got weirder. He showed me the house, but all day it felt like a business meeting, like he was trying to sell it to me or something. But on the way around I saw two things, two statues that belonged to me and Boon."

Dara, who'd been listening with an open mouth, cocked her head. "Could they have been similar?"

"No." Felix said, telling her enough without the details, "one of them we lost on the way here. I've never seen anything like it."

Now Dara was also stumped. They looked at each other, the squid grew cold. A moth landed on the coffee table, scuttled around for a moment, and then took off again.

"What then?"

"Well, we just acted like everything was all right, like he was my dad and was happy to see me. But I know he was lying."

"What do you mean?"

"Gut feelings. I can't imagine why someone would lie about this, logically. But it didn't feel right."

They were about to fall into a silent spell again, when Dara caught sight of the pink sky outside. It was nearly sunset. "Where is Boon?"

Felix didn't answer, but shrugged his shoulders. He looked lost, standing there running his hands over the nape of his neck. When he came to no conclusion, he sat down next to her again, staring at the window where a golden ray of sun was thinning to a slit. He could smell the rosemary soap on her.

"What do you think?" he asked quietly.

"About Boon?"

He nodded.

"I don't know. I wish I'd asked for a name."

Felix sighed. "What do you think he's gotten himself into?"

She pressed her palms into her eyes. "He said "Goaty, I'm sorry."" After repeating it to herself for so long, she remembered every inflection in his voice. "Just like that."

Felix caught her eye. He held his breath as some steps approached, quickened, and then went past the house. He shook his head again and let it fall onto the couch behind him.

"I don't know, Dara. It just doesn't sound like Boon."

Chapter 15

SINKING BACK INTO THE SHADOWS of the houses, Boon should have felt like a spy. The night market buzzed with movement and colors, each stall decorated and set up under a bright tent overflowing with trinkets and food. Even from the periphery of the street, he could see the piles of clothes, fruit and Japanese toys peeking over the thick crowd of people. There were sun hats and belts hanging from hooks and jeweled necklaces catching the light in giddy pirouettes. He only stopped once, craning his neck to see a stall covered in box upon box of stuff: CDs and DVDs, action movies, rock music, whole entire TV shows, novels and comic books—Thai, Chinese, English—a foreign section and a place for novelties. It took up three tables and had ten men manning it, some shouting prices, some giving recommendations, and three, joined at the shoulders, swaying, singing nondescript words to a Stevie Ray Vaughan song. Boon wiped his sweaty palms on his pants. It was a commendable stall.

Boon advanced with as much stealth as he could muster all along the market until he reached the agreed location, a bubblegum pink hairdresser with fake eucalyptus vines climbing up the front. But even with the wild excitement of the night, and his own mission, a combination that would've normally brought a secret smile to his lips, Boon was on edge. He had the money in a thick envelope in his suit's breast pocket, and he patted it uncertainly, like he had done repeatedly throughout the day. After everything he and Felix had been through, he was surprised that he'd managed to keep the cash. Just before winning at poker, and getting through the trip, he had been tempted to come clean about his plan.

That was another thing that made him jumpy. There were few things he kept to himself, and Felix could sense a lie with his eyes closed. He hoped that, by keeping quiet, he hadn't given anything away.

When it came to it, it would be a difficult thing to explain. Why was he buying a fake passport for his brother? And *how* exactly was it legal? He was a marketing man, much less savvy on the ways of reason than those of persuasion. He came up with the ideas without too much concern for details. At the market, he waited without knowing who he was supposed to meet. All the time he patted the pocket self-consciously and strained his ears for when his conscience came to call.

Eventually, he felt a tap on his shoulder and jolted from the surprise. A vulpine man was standing to his right, arms crossed, looking out into the street. Boon guessed this was to pretend that, from afar, they would seem like good friends enjoying the evening, and not, he thought while pulling the collar of his shirt loose around his neck, suspicious at all.

"How do we start?" he said, whispering for the first time in his life.

"Well firstly," the man said, the corners of his mouth turning up around his canines, "you say hello."

"Right." Boon was already sweating. The man, on the other hand, had an impenetrable calm. "Right."

"Call me Joe."

Joe was speaking from the corner of his mouth, so that again, Boon guessed, people passing would assume the two friends were staring ahead in silence.

"Do you have the money?"

"Yes." Boon reached self-consciously and tapped his pocket. "Do you have the thing?"

"The passport? Of course I have it." He looked at Boon then, and raised his eyebrows. In the semi-light he seemed young, his features sharp. "That *is* why you came."

Boon kept quiet. Having worn himself thin with worry, he was surprised at Joe's ability to make a joke at such a time. But it was his job after all. He waited for more instructions, tearing a plastic eucalyptus leaf to bits to keep his hands busy.

Eventually, Joe spoke again.

"When I say so, take out the money, and don't make a big deal out of it. I have the passport here in my hand. When I say, I'll give it to you and you hand me the money. Relaxed. No false moves, alright?"

Again, Boon was impressed. He didn't expect the deal to go so—well—nicely. He gradually stopped shaking as much.

"Ok. Now."

All around them, the market bustle continued with new waves of tourists and shoppers milling about, celebrating under the same twinkling lights the men made the exchange.

As soon as both had grabbed and let go of the appropriate things, Joe gave a small nod, and stepped slightly away from Boon, as if suddenly afraid he would snatch the envelope back.

"I need not warn you what will happen if not all the money's in here?"

"No. It's all there. Don't worry."

"I'm not worried." Joe said, all controlled and serious, before stepping further into the shadow of the store. "Good doing business with you."

And just like that, he was gone.

Boon stood there, half mystified, half smug. For some time, he let himself enjoy the warmth of the night, the rich smells traveling along the main road, and the colors of the spring. He was proud of himself, for what he'd pulled off, but unfortunately he should have reveled in the feeling longer, because when he opened the passport at last, his excitement dissipated as quickly as it had come.

Back in New York when he'd first set up the deal, he had sent them his brother's picture, taken when he was sitting with a table of friends. It wasn't a picture that could've been used for the passport, but the fake was supposed to look enough like his brother to pass. However, now he stared at the passport with a feeling of dread. It wasn't just that the man in the passport didn't look like his brother at all. The bigger problem was that the picture looked like someone else entirely, because it was a photo of Felix.

It was late, however, and he realized there was loud music and screams coming from somewhere in the market. He had a headache. He couldn't remember if he'd drunk anything beforehand. Looking around himself, he didn't know *what* to feel, so he opened up the passport again, then again, and then put it in his pocket until the next day, when hopefully, he could think more clearly. Maybe it was his conscience catching up after all.

For the first time that night, he acted calmly. He secured the package, straightened his jacket and headed, finally, home. He started whistling, a tuneless song. He didn't know if he would ever understand how this had happened. The possibility of Felix's face on the passport—maybe, maybe it would change in the morning, he thought. Maybe he would make sense of it after a good night's sleep and a couple of aspirins— how he missed his aspirins. Maybe only then. *How could he have Felix's passport?* The road turned left, away from all the noise and confusion of the city.

All with time. All with time.

Felix cursed Boon with each heavy step he took. He was traveling a deserted road on the hottest day in Phuket, headed toward Boon's brother's home, alone. Boon had come in late the night before, acting funny. He had looked at Felix as strangely as Felix had returned the look, both on the edge of saying something or waiting for the other to, until, exhausted, they had fallen asleep. But Boon hadn't been drunk. He had moved with caution, with less swagger than usual. And he had been the first to wake up. In fact, they were supposed to make the trek to his brother's house together, the whole five miles uphill, but he had excused himself soon after breakfast and had taken a walk to think. *To think!*

In the meantime, Felix stumbled over another mangrove root. The path had turned sandy, and it formed hills over the twisting vegetation beneath. With the trees closing in and pools of water appearing in cutouts of the earth, the air seemed to get more dense, compressed with humidity and shadow; that is until, walking further into the thicket, the mangroves began to spread out again and Felix emerged from the mangal onto the sea. He took a moment to catch his breath and stretch his neck as he looked at the new landscape. In front of him, crystalline water and wooden houses on stilts.

"To think about what?" he mumbled to himself, and started heading toward the village.

Felix had learnt early on that it was impossible to ever see right through Boon. In fact, he would find out many things about his friends by talking to his parents—how he was allergic to kiwis or that he had learnt a Flemish poem for his mother's fortieth birthday. It was hard to believe that with his manicured nails he had once worked the blueberries fields in New Jersey, or that he had won a ticket to the White House Easter Egg Roll with a call-in at NPR when he was six. One only got to know Boon when he wished to let it happen. Regardless, he was a man of logic, and Felix generally understood him better than anyone else.

Neither he nor Dara, however, could figure where he'd gone that morning. Normally, eager for conversation, it was unlike him to evade company. Or, Felix thought, rubbing his jaw, maybe not. After all, it was also unlike him to mess with money and receive strange calls. Boon had some nerve to send him to his brother's alone. This visit wasn't his greatest worry at the moment. Scanning the shanty, stilted houses, he didn't even know if he'd reached the right place.

When it came to it, there were few things that Tao was afraid of.

He was a straightforward man who had taken a job as a fisherman right out of school. He had never been very ambitious, but unlike some of the boys in his class, who had tried to get a say in lofty careers, he had considered few other options and pursued his future with leisure. He was, perhaps, the best kind of fisherman too—in the good seasons, when the shrimp were copious and the bass healthy, he would try a hand at cooking and invite his neighbors over, tossing generous scraps to stray dogs and the seagulls that would perch on his deck in the morning. And when the sea ate the wooden poles of the house while he starved on bananas and steamed fig leaves, he slept fitfully and cast his hope out with the lines, for those were the bad seasons. But always, he was fascinated by the sea.

Even of the tides, licking at the foundations of his home, he wasn't afraid. He knew there would be a time when the structure would collapse, and he would have to find another place to live. But in the meantime, he took care of his home the way a wounded man nurses his injury. He didn't have much imagination, but filled the rooms with carvings of animals or fish he would see out on the boat—the footrests he modeled after the sea turtles that lived in the bay, while pegged to the walls were featherbacks and carps, moorish idols, surgeonfish, a long moray eel. The bowls were fashioned like the underside of puffers and the trivet for his wok and saucepan like a manta ray, fitted with a leather strap for the tail.

When the house would end up in the sea, only then, he intended to move.

The last time he had really felt afraid was during the first episode. It was a rarity for him not to feel well, especially in May, so he had decided to stay at home to work on repairing the kitchen window. He was halfway done when the pain took him, a severe tightness in his abdomen that gradually spread to his back and shoulders. He was still young: a thirty-seven year old shouldn't be breaking into a fever, hunched over the sink, because of nothing. But come evening, when attempts at eating and drinking had worsened the pain, and he had little to distract himself from it, he had gone to the hospital. After learning about the disease, *Pancreatitis*, the subsequent episodes that would come throughout the year became part of his life. Fear, he thought, came from fantasizing things happening. Once told something, true that is, he fully embraced it. Then, there was no point in being afraid—of what? he would ask Annop and Navin when he reached their boats out at sea on a particularly ugly day. Usually, they would just shake their heads and toss him a flask of hot tea, he would read them the forecast, and they would fish. The worry was left behind in the shacks, over a bottle of Hong Thong whiskey and fish scales stripped clean. With its beauty and temper, the Andaman Sea took all his worries away.

When Felix reached the stilted house right on the edge of the beach, grabbing a wooden knocker carved into a mean barracuda, both him and Tao were in a foul mood.

Tao had just begun brewing tea when the knock came. It upset him that he should have to stay at home on such a beautiful day to mend his lines, and visitors would slow him down. The boy had a curious expression, something dark and brooding and contemplative, but he was taking too long to unlace his shoes so Tao left him on the threshold and went back into the kitchen to sew. After a while, he heard the door shutting and a moment later the boy appeared in the doorway.

"Is this going to take a while or are you passing?" Tao said without looking up from his work.

"Are you going out?"

"No," Tao replied, sighing, "but then you'd better make tea, if you kindly would."

The water was about to boil over, so Felix hurried around the kitchen looking for the cups and tea leaves without a word from the man. Felix was still angry at Boon, and only lit up when he went to place the steeping cups on the ray trivet.

"Did you make this?"

Tao glanced up over the mess of the net. "Took me a month."

"And these?" Felix held up his teacup, a coral wrapped around the handle.

"Took me about two months for all eight."

Felix walked to stand behind Tao's chair and picked something off the counter. Something, judging by the clinking of the spoon on the metal inside, that must've been the sugar bowl.

Without turning, Tao said, "Took me a month just to fit it with that steel-lining. I forgot to ask if you drink your tea sweet."

Felix circled back around and looked at the coral cups again. "What took you the longest?"

"I don't know."

"You mean you don't keep count?"

Tao sighed. He had never been an entertainer of guests, neither was he preoccupied with showing off.

"Probably the helm of my boat. It's very heavy, sometimes inconveniently so. But it's beautiful. I modeled it off the Buddhist wheel of dharma, but with a different animal at each handle."

"Are you a Buddhist?"

"No."

"Are you religious?"

"Every fisherman needs something." Tao said, sucking on his thumb where the needle had pricked him.

"Why?"

"Otherwise he would switch jobs."

Felix stopped looking out the window to the sea and faced Tao, who had gone back to work. "I get that."

Tao raised his eyebrows. "Good. Now," he said, taking a sip of tea, "would you care to explain why you're here?"

Felix's cheeks reddened and he quickly gave a wai. It hadn't even occurred to him to check if he had found the right house.

"My name is Felix, I've come from Phuket. Are you Boon-Mee's brother?"

For the first time, Tao gave the boy a good look. In his surprise, Felix had lost the anger and stared back with curiosity. Evidently, there had been something on his mind before. But there was something else that surfaced when his mask slipped. Alongside the birthmark under his eye, it was an expression Tao had seen before.

"Yeah, I'm Tao. We've never met?"

"I don't think so."

"And you also come from New York?"

"Yes." Felix said, sitting down at last.

Tao shrugged. There were many names and people and fish in his mind and who knows where he had seen that face before. "I heard the journey was difficult."

Dara's way of picking up details had rubbed off on Felix. "Has Boon been here already?"

"No. He just called a couple of times. He told me about Paris."

"Right."

Tao was now the curious one. He hadn't heard much from Boon since their arrival to Thailand. He wanted to know if Boon had gotten the passport after all. Maybe, Felix was here to relay information.

"Everything else went smoothly?"

"We made it here."

"And after that?" Tao said, keeping his eyes lowered and his hands busy. He had stopped sewing the net some time ago but fiddled with a knot.

Felix frowned. "I guess we've been having fun."

Tao didn't push it. He took a break to drink the tea and look at Felix to try and answer his other question. He had seen him before, he remembered the light stain from somewhere that was not exactly the face in front of him. Not for a while now, but Tao felt like he had known the boy. Tao poured himself another cup of tea and continued to stare. The room had fallen silent, and Felix felt uneasy at the sudden interest in him.

"What?" he said, laughing the tension off.

But Tao narrowed his eyes and peered closer at him. "I've seen you before."

Another odd response. Both Boon and Tao had expressive faces they couldn't control in common. That and their extreme vagueness. Felix felt some of his previous gloom return.

"Where?"

But it was just as Tao's forehead cleared and he was about to answer that the front door opened and Boon came marching into the kitchen, holding a long white package in his hands.

After setting it down on the counter and drinking a glass of water, he spun to look at them. He had a crazed expression.

Tao got up first. "Brother."

The two hadn't seen each other since Boon had been a teenager, when his family had left Thailand for good. Because of the age gap, they'd never been close, but they embraced for the second time in their life with the joy of knowing they were family. Then, Tao approached the package and Boon went about making himself a cup of tea.

"What'd you bring me? Tuna? To a fisherman?"

The fish itself was an odd color, and smelt pretty bad too. But Tao cleaned and seasoned it and wrapped the pieces in aluminum foil before placing it in the oven. On the stove, he started making rice. The kitchen was quiet for some time. It wasn't until Tao was satisfied with the preparations of lunch and had set out plates and the food that he turned around and gave Boon a look. He poured himself fresh tea.

"So," he said, sipping from the steaming cup, smirking a little, "do you have it?"

Boon glanced at Felix. He got up, grabbed four beers from the fridge and set one down in front of each of them and two in front of himself. He drained one in a couple of gulps. Both men were looking at him strangely.

"You haven't told him have you?" Tao said, twisting his own cap loose.

"No."

Felix had a curious capacity for patience. He got up to open the window, for it had gotten hot with the oven turned on, took a couple of careful sips from his own beer and cracked his knuckles all before Boon spoke.

Surprisingly, it was easier explaining to Felix that it had been to himself.

"It's real simple," Boon started, popping an aspirin into his second beer, "Tao has had acute pancreatitis for a year or so, and the surgery to cure it is tricky. But left unattended is not an option. So I proposed he come to the United States to get it fixed."

He treaded around his words in a way Felix had never seen him do before. Marketing men normally spoke with a certainty known only to themselves.

"And you need a passport to travel." Tao was finding the whole thing a bit dramatic, and tried to expedite the process. "So we needed a fake passport."

"Why fake?" asked Felix.

"I'm getting to that." Boon said. "When our mother was pregnant with Tao, our parents decided that China had better prospects, so they got jobs there, working in Beijing. In the meantime, Tao was born."

"So I'm a Chinese citizen." Tao said, ignoring a look from Boon.

"Not exactly. He got a Chinese birth certificate, and would've been a Thai citizen had he gotten the documents straightened out when my parents moved back to Phuket. But now, with our parents in New York, and Tao living here for so long without any type of formal process to say he was born to Thai parents, it's harder to prove he isn't Chinese."

"And I've no proof to say I've lived here for five years either, no bank account, no bills. So without being a citizen, I would have to sort that out too before applying for a passport, which I would have to do as a Chinese person." The speech sounded well-rehearsed and foreign coming from Tao.

"And you can't live years with pancreatitis without getting it cured." Boon said, shooting Tao a look. "Here the hospitals aren't so great."

With the story over, Tao got up to take the fish out of the oven, and Felix moved the nets away from the table to make room. But Tao didn't place the tray down immediately.

"Boon?" Tao said with a curt smile. "Now, bringing fish to a sailor's home isn't the worst offense, but bringing rotten fish might be."

The meat was gray and putrid. Even Felix, who had been taken by the story, had secretly found the smell foul in the heat.

"Where did you get this?" Tao asked, inspecting it.

"The Sea Gypsy market." Boon said. "They said it was caught this morning."

"Well," Tao said, looking at the thing one last time, "there's no point in making the sauce now."

He grabbed the pan in his left hand, pushed aside the curtains and window panes so no oil would get on them, and threw the whole thing down into the water. He washed the container to get rid of the smell, and picked up a *nam man hoi* bottle to drizzle on top of the steaming white rice. While it was no tuna steak, the oyster-sauce had a flavor incomparable to anything Felix had had before.

Taking big mouthfuls, Felix said finally, "Alright, so that's what you've been sneaking off to do for the past weeks."

"Yes."

"That's the big secret." Tao said, smirking.

Boon, nauseous by the fish, the story and diet of painkillers, excused himself to smoke a cigarette. Tao gathered the plates, rinsed them, grabbed a carving knife, the one that didn't make his thumb so sore, and took up a half-formed nurse shark talisman and its clamp stand.

Felix didn't know what to do with himself. He made some more tea, even if he didn't want any; he thought about joining Boon but remained sitting, taking up the nets in his hand and twirling a line around his finger until the tip became purple. With everyone quiet, he noticed a loud clock on the wall, a brightly painted oriental whip snake eating his own tail. He didn't bother reading the time. Right then, he didn't want to think about what they had to do, what time they would get back to Dara or, even more, his meeting with his father. He sighed—Boon had many bad habits, but as he reached into his coat pocket for an aspirin, he was grateful for every single one. Well, save, of course, for forgetfulness.

"Boon," Felix felt his anger come back—he remembered the previous day's phone call. "I thought we were even now."

When Boon came rushing back, he had no breath in him at all. He saw the passport in Felix's hand and flinched. "Right. Except for this."

"Is this the fake?" Tao asked, and when Boon nodded he frowned, "That's Felix."

"Better yet, who was the guy who you hired to mug us?" Felix said. He grabbed two beers, approached Boon, flipped the caps onto the floor and shoved one into Boon's hand. "He called yesterday, by the way."

"He did?"

"Passed his regards in fact. Cheers."

Boon didn't want to drink, the facts were foggy enough, but he held the bottle tightly with both hands. "Who?"

"You're joking."

"No."

Felix gave a short laugh. "You mean you don't know?"

"No."

Tao was also getting worked up now. If there is one thing he disliked about his brother it was how convoluted he made things to be. "Boon, what business have you gotten yourself into?"

"First of all, I've been planning this a lot sooner than our trip to Paris. I called an agency that deals with this stuff way back, and yesterday, when I met to make the deal, I was given this. I don't know how." He placed two cold fingers to his left temple—he was getting a headache. "I have no idea."

"You've never seen the man then?" Tao said, thoughtfully.

Boon shook his head and replayed the whole thing in his head; from the moment he had called the sketchy number in New York, describing Tao's appearance, to the subsequent phone calls to arrange the meeting, to the deal itself, Boon had never had a good feeling about this.

Felix on the other hand was preoccupied with something else. "The man who called, he asked for you specifically. He knew where you were staying."

"He called at Dara's house?"

"He told her to pass on a message." Felix said, "It was "Goaty, I'm sorry." He said he stole the money and passports and that he didn't have them now. Well, one of the passports is here—"

But Felix had caught the change in Boon's face, not just because it was an odd message—no—it meant something to him. Before he could say something Boon spoke.

"*Goaty,* that's what he said?"

"Yes."

"Well that's odd." And for the first time Boon almost smiled, "because that's what George used to call me when we were kids."

This affected Tao as well. "George—cousin George? In Paris?"

"Yes. I don't understand why he would steal from us." Boon said. "He wouldn't get involved in that type of work. I wouldn't think so anyway, I mean, he's not that sharp."

At this Felix chuckled. He held his beer up and drank, and for the first time in a while, so did Boon. They were confused, all three of them, but Boon's pulse had slowed. With the truth out, he felt at ease again. Felix smiled at him.

Actually, Felix laughed a hearty laugh—he was prone to do that when situations got more ridiculous still. "I met my dad yesterday."

While Tao frowned, Boon's face lit up. He was glad for a change in topic. "Right! How did it go?"

"Well, you know," he started, and had to laugh again at his next words, "I don't think he was my real father even though he said he was."

Boon shook his head. "I don't follow."

"He knew about the fax I'd sent, saying I was his son coming to visit, but it seemed like he was testing me, or waiting for me to say something." Again, Felix searched the ceiling for an explanation. "Then when I was about to leave he said he was my father. I had no memories of the place, or him." He thought back to his visit, only yesterday, and his laughter died down. "And the weirdest part is that, Boon, he had the chameleon. Aunt Vivi's chameleon! And the angel statuette. Had them both propped up in his house. I just don't understand it."

"Maybe he was the same boy that sold me the passport? What did he look like?"

"He was huge. I've never seen anyone like him. Right out of a movie—shifty little eyes and a big beard that hid his mouth. His name is Shyuri, and I thought he had it tattooed to his arm but when I looked closer it said "Rafflesia," it's a type of flower. He had tattoos all over his chest actually—"

Tao had retreated in a corner to carve, as he had felt that the conversation did not relate to him. Now, however, he looked up from his work and spoke.

"Maybe he was or is part of a gang. They're a real thing here, in Thailand. Normally members are 'branded' with some sort of symbol. Boon—"

But Boon had also thought of something. "The man I met yesterday also had a 'Rafflesia' tattoo. Right on his forearm?" And when Felix nodded he continued, "I thought I'd seen it before—"

It wasn't until Boon had said it that Felix remembered the man with whom they'd played poker on the train. On his wrist, in blocky letters, had been the word. "What does this mean?"

Boon clicked his tongue and held his beer tight. Felix took a sip of his—how did Shyuri have the chameleon? *Why had he pretended to be his father?*

Again, Tao had been listening quietly, and had let the afternoon stumble to its senses without approaching a particular thought, that now, however, resurfaced.

"Felix, I'm sure I've seen you before."

"Right." Felix was still thinking over the various facts of the previous two days to really catch what Tao was saying. "Maybe I was walking in the street somewhere?"

"No, what I mean to say is that I knew you. When you were little." Tao pointed to Felix's birthmark. "I remember you from elementary school."

Both Felix and Boon turned to stare at him.

"Right after I left Phuket's fisherman's coalition—the year I was figuring out the solo business, when I was twenty-two, I used to help out during the soccer season. You were in first grade. I taught you how to do a stepover. I know where you used to live. I can show you if you want."

Chapter 16

IT ALL STARTED TO COME back when they passed through the elementary school courtyard and took a break by the water fountains on the side of the gym. Felix tried to catch glimpses of the past; a droplet of sweat that itched behind the knee, little scratches in a music CD that he swore would play from a bench at recess. But it was hard to distinguish what he really did remember—like the particular lock of the gate that took two tries to open—from what could have been. It was almost too easy to imagine himself there, five years old, scraping his knees on the concrete steps up into the schoolhouse or pressing his palms to the hot, black window sills until one of the boys in the circle pulled back first.

During his time in Thailand, perhaps, more than moments, it was feelings that he remembered—slipping on the puddled condolences of August into a hellish September, when the soybean fields reeked of growth and heat swelled the cities. Or, his finger on the catch of a lighter and *grab the float!* and, behold, a whole lake of paper lanterns for Loy Krathong in

November. Then, he remembered how the last few windy days in March, before a two-month break, brought a great sleepiness in the school and the children would lay in rows under the sea mango trees and, like all children in the world, found shapes in the clouds.

"And there," Tao said, pointing to a little hut at the corner of the courtyard, "is the soccer shed. I used to let the littlies, preschool kids like you, carry the ball and cones and set up the court. You ran around like crazy while all the older kids warmed up."

Felix smiled as if it were his own memory.

A short way from the school, the rusty-water taste still in their mouths, they reached the point where the paved road inclined sharply, sticky with mud that clung to your shoes during monsoons. They walked past it and past some papaya trees that bore no fruit, as far as Tao could remember, and finally arrived at a standstill. They faced three houses built up on the little hill, two older structures and a brand new one with shiny windows and black and white walls. Tao led him toward one of the older houses on the right.

With the same imprecision with which he remembered anything about Thailand, Felix recognized the house. When they had turned away from the city and ventured up the path, he had been stopped short by the smell of wild orchids that grew, first in small clusters and then in heavy columns, out from the ferns and undergrowth that lined the way. The scent was cinnamon and vanilla and familiar. The steps up to the front door too—first a couple, then a patch of basil, and then three more—were a rhythm he had walked before. Unlike Shyuri's house, he felt like he had been here. But when they reached the door, a small golden plate nailed to the wall caught his eye.

"*Massage and Yoga,*" Tao read out loud. He frowned and looked at the other two houses in the clearing, scraping some dust from his boots and rubbing his hands together. "Look, maybe I'm mistaken."

But Felix shook his head—he knew the place. He took a breath and reached for the handle, grinning at Tao with more confidence than he really had. "Why not?" And he opened the door before he was ready for it.

Inside, they entered a large sitting room with two couches and a large Japanese ink painting on the wall. It was very bright with ultraviolet light, so much so that Felix noticed, for the first time, a light scar on Tao's right temple. Not long after appeared a young girl with pearly skin and a pink uniform who bowed and presented them with a plate of coconut puddings, each a colorful dome. Tao had to nudge Felix in the ribs to remind him to bow back.

"Do you have an appointment?" She said, ready to lead them to a studio without an answer.

Still peering at her neatly pinned back hair and the creamy rug they stood on, Felix grinned. With his sweaty brow and scent of fish, he felt out of place. "No, we don't," said Felix.

He thought about his next words. "I used to live here when I was a little boy, I haven't been here since. I'm looking for my family and I was hoping you could help us out."

Her eyes were wide, but she nodded politely. She too seemed to choose how to answer.

"This place opened seven years ago. We don't have any information about the previous owners on file if that's what you're looking for. I never met the family." She clicked her tongue, and offered them the puddings again. "I'm sorry about that sir."

Felix smiled and nodded back. He finally took a perfectly pink pudding and stood poised with it resting between his fingers, holding his breath. He could feel Tao's eyes on him.

"That's fine, thank you anyways. Is it alright if we sit down for a moment?" he said, gesturing toward the couches.

The girl's forehead cleared. She nodded again, set the plate on the table and with a final bow, retreated to a room in the back—they heard the sound of a CD clicking in and music playing. The room smelled faintly of the orchids and sandalwood that was burning on a little brass dish by the window.

"Felix." Tao said, looking at his hands.

But Felix's mind had been working since they read the sign outside. In fact, since the previous day's adventure.

"My family isn't here. But this is where I grew up. I remember the house." He was surprised at how easily he said it, and took a bite from the pink dome.

Tao winced, as if he hadn't been thinking the same. But Felix's expressions had changed. He was squishing gently on the coconut jelly, his jaw tense. He glanced at the sun rays hitting the wall panels and took another whiff of orchid and wood. You can never really forget a scent. He was sure.

"What I don't understand is why Shyuri pretended to be my father. I've never been to that place or seen the man before." he locked eyes with Tao and tried to find the connection. "How on earth did he have our things?"

Tao didn't have an answer, so Felix just shook his head again and let the confusion of the day wash over him. He was exhausted. With the same tattoo as the man Boon traded with and San'ya, if that was even his real name, Shyuri was most definitely involved in something ugly, and by messing around, so were they now. Just then, the girl popped her head around the door and gave a little start to see them still waiting in the shop, but she disappeared without saying a word. In the pink anonymity of the room, he could almost imagine getting home to Dara and another curry dinner dropped off by Khun Ao, Yai pouring tea for everyone and spilling it just twice. Felix wanted to call after the girl and her neat hands, the way she could take all this wretched business and straighten it out like freshly-printed newspaper.

Chapter 17

IT WAS ODD, FELIX THOUGHT, how some people just don't cry —not at weddings, not at the movies, and not, as he was about to find out, in the face of death. He had not grown fond of Dara's father during their brief visit to the temple, and had thought little of him since. But it felt wrong that his passing should bring no grief onto the world. Luang Pho Sunan died on a balmy Tuesday afternoon and stubbing her toes on the coffin brought more tears to Dara than seeing her father lay inside it.

But Dara rolled her eyes when Felix half-joked, half-frowned at her for it.

"What about Aunt Mertha?" she asked, recalling a recent conversation about how horrible she was.

"I did *love* Aunt Mertha." he said, popping the word like a balloon.

"From what you told me she sounded *awful*."

"She was. But I loved her, in a way." Felix said, surprising himself again. Dara nodded slowly, but raised an eyebrow, challenging him.

"Were you sad when she died?"

This he pondered for a moment. It was complicated, she was family.

"No."

Dara smiled, kissed him on the cheek, and skipped out the door in her purple gown, the Thai color of death, Felix head to toe in black himself. He thought about Nelson and choked up, pulling his collar looser around his neck. "It's not the same," he muttered, taking a deep breath, before following her out.

True, when Aunt Mertha died he was just short of celebrating with Zion, beers and cheers and all. But there was a muted respect for Hercules as they passed him in the hallway —Felix would smile and shake his head at the memory of her, big and sticky and his only aunt. Perhaps, he considered as he headed to the funeral two days later, muted respect was all that Sunan would get. It was a bleaker sort of mourning—a silence borne out of lack of good things to say rather than sadness. But it put Felix at ease—it was solemn nonetheless.

They paused their scheming for a week. After their visit to the Spa house, the four had been brainstorming possibilities and going over the events of their trip—the mugging, the poker game, the impossible coincidences they'd found—with Yai bringing them unevenly cut mangoes and glasses of cold water.

Their loud discussions and confused despair went quiet the moment Dara received the telegram from the temple. No one dared bring up the subject of Shyuri or the money in question anymore, and when Dara tried to mention the case during the funeral Boon ignored it: if she wasn't going to mourn, they would do it for her.

Individually, however, everyone remained secretly busy. Boon went to the library and studied the history of tattoos. He read about Indian ink, cadmium, cobalt, dichromate salts and all that there was to be read of gang signs and the local branches of the practice. The only one among the four with a tattoo, it made sense for him to take up the subject. He also called George, whose story confirmed their theory.

"Two thugs ambushed him in a bar, beat him up and stole the satchel with the money and passports. He said they were right low-life criminals, and aggressive too. They said they knew you and wanted to take a look at your passport." Boon raised his eyebrows and put on a tone, though Felix couldn't quite pin it. "George defended your honor until they reduced him to a bloody pulp."

Felix had snickered at the story, but the fact remained: they had *known* him, they had followed George and, most importantly, the men had been Thai.

Tao returned to his house and looked into the passport trade instead. It was slower work, going to meet the older fishermen—men he knew had dabbled in black markets and were the core of Phuket's underground fights—but they were the only lead he could think of. They were weary of questions, men with morals led by fear, and for that reason, Tao had to be careful himself, lest he gave too much information or showed too much interest in the things he was told. Truth is, he was interested. If he didn't get out now, with Boon and a fake ID, he feared he never would. The men acted slowly, reluctantly, but with patience learned from being on the water, so did he.

Felix, being the most upset about the whole thing, took a direct course of action. He went into the best place he knew, a place that would spill information through gossip, bribery, or drunken loquaciousness the fastest. In the bar, a couple of drinks offered by him, he heard bits and pieces about Shyuri, or a man fit for his size and meanness. But the crowd itself wasn't eager to talk and, because of Shyuri's reclusiveness, there wasn't much to talk about.

Only when a man approached him on his way out did Felix hear anything worth the 200 baht he had spent on drinks in exchange for information.

"He comes downtown every Thursday morning to the garden center and has bags of fertilizer sent to his house." the man started, raising his eyebrows, "I go to the center very often. I have an orchard, and I'm always running in and out. But he takes his time there. Occasionally I've seen him linger in the shop for hours at a time. I've never talked to him, no, except maybe one time when he was leaving and I gave him directions to this new shrimp eatery. I'm not sure where he goes afterward, but I'll bet he likes good food as much as plants. You can try asking around the restaurant district, maybe someone there knows him."

Dara was the only one who couldn't go about working on their mission without the others telling her to take it easy. It was very hypocritical, she thought, for them to distract themselves with their plans and for her to have to sit in her house like a porcelain doll. She knew they were itching to get back into the planning, but as guests and friends, she also knew that it was the only thing that was *right* for them to do. So as they ran about the place, avoiding questions about each other's whereabouts, brimming with information they had to wait to tell, she thought—she thought about her father, and then Felix's almost father, and his tattoos.

She had known many boys in her class that would skip days of school and come back men, black ink and red skin, decorated like the prettiest birthday cakes. They showed their tattoos to each other, raising their shirts high and causing all the girls to giggle. Dara too had been fascinated by them. Boys with the same drawings walked together, talked with their eyes. The deliciousness of a secret. She had never considered whether she liked tattoos much, but with so much time alone, she mused on the possibility of it.

Each day, the evening approached reluctantly, as if waiting for her friends to return home before pooling shadows on the emerging critters and low lives of the city. Yai stayed with her, playing with the house geckos and afternoon light. He was learning how to read and would sit with piles of books and magazines stacked around him, running his fingers over clusters of words, sounding each one out decisively. When he couldn't quite understand it, she would write the syllables on her hand and show it to him.

"In-du-stry. Industry." he repeated over and over, turning his head from a fresh mark on her hand toward the book and then back again. "In-du-stry."

All up her arm was smudged with the ink, and she rubbed spit in it as Yai laid back down again, bare-back, onto the floor, resuming his exercises. She looked at his shoulder blades poking out behind him and the sun coming in at a slant. She got up, put sunscreen on his cheeks and sat back down again. It wasn't hard to decide if she liked tattoos after all.

Her confinement ended when, around a week later, she went to pick flowers for her father to be planted in the temple in his memory. All three boys tagged along, Tao in the lead with her, and Boon and Felix carrying Yai on their shoulders behind. It was a welcome distraction for Dara and she took her time choosing the arrangement. Whether she was trying to honor her father with the most vivid plant, or even her mother, with her meticulous eye for beauty, the boys didn't know. But she raked up and down the flower shop's small aisles, and then the garden behind, taking her first wonderful breath of April.

Phuket, an undeniably big city, offered many occasions for coincidence. While the five of them compared plants, only a couple of streets away, a lilac house with sea-glass dreamcatchers hung above the doors was being ransacked. Two men, one smoking, one fiddling with the blade of a spearpoint knife, rifled through drawers and kitchen cabinets and underneath a little boy's bed. What they had come to find was not there, they agreed, looking at the circle of mystery novels on the floor, but they lingered nonetheless. They were hot and tired of running around. With a thick black marker, the two started drawing on the living room window. Neither was a masterful artist, and yet they could copy the image exactly. Slowly, the form of a rafflesia began to appear on the glass and grow bigger and bigger the more they added to it—an April Fool's joke it was, what Felix and his friends might call a *coincidence* later, something that would surely make the Big Man smile.

When he would be telling Selena and Nelson about the trip, Felix did not mention the motorcycle. It was in fact a three wheeled vehicle with no passenger doors, resembling the

Italian APE 50 or Indian rickshaws—*fundamentally*, Felix thought the first time he saw one, *a tuk tuk is a cross between a motorcycle and a milk van, and more uncomfortable than both*. It came about his life through Tao. Alongside fishing poles and old nets he never got round to repairing, he had had a tuk tuk stored in his fisherman shed, bought when, among the list of things he had tried his hand at, Tao had decided to become a taxi driver. A lonesome spirit with little patience for noise, he had hated it. So it was a surprise to both himself and Felix to be trotting along in it down the winding roads of Thailand's countryside headed past the most wonderful landscapes toward Shyuri's house.

Because it had been abandoned fifteen years ago, and left to degrade in the salty-humid environment that eats everything in a fisherman's house, the tuk tuk had considerable problems. Felix had to sit on a plastic crate tied to the structure with rope, and had to hold part of the windshield, dislodged from the frame, lest it fell out. Tao himself had to make sure the gear wouldn't disengage each time they passed over a bump in the road, which was often, or that the brake pedal wouldn't get jammed with the rust. The entire way to the house, with banana and papaya trees lining the road and the lake glimmering in the morning light, they drove mostly in silence, straining their ears for the sound of the motor giving out.

Felix had also kept this visit from his parents for the most obvious reason. After returning home from the flower shop to the break-in, the four had wasted no more time. After all, they had been too lucky already: a group of kids, they had written their rough plans on napkins that they carried in their pockets —something done purely out of convenience but that had left no trace when the robbers had raided the house. Robbers or, most likely, gang members. Someone was after them, and now, it wasn't only himself and Boon that were caught up with the rafflesia business, but Tao, Dara and Yai.

Returning to Shyuri's house was something Felix wasn't excited about. It was a Thursday, and he was hoping that the bar man had been truthful about Shyuri going to the garden center in the morning. When he had asked around the restaurant district, many owners had claimed that a man of his description often stayed in town as late as four in the afternoon. Still, Felix wasn't exactly planning on staying that long. After all, the five of them had little time left before their getaway.

They were nearing the house now. He could smell the hot perfume of the flowers that grew best in the quiet wilderness of the country. In his pocket was the napkin with the final plan:

1. Find out who Shyuri was
2. Search for Boon's passport
3. Steal back the chameleon

It was not a plan the secret service would be proud of, but a practical one for that.

When Boon had called George, he had also inquired about the statues. Two men had indeed robbed him of the passports and money, but he didn't know anything about the chameleon except that Boon had pawned it and he had intended to steal their money and buy it back. George had seen it propped up in his mother's glass display since he was a little boy, and its absence was a blow. He had also been jealous that Vivi gave a gift to Boon, and still was, but, the gentleman he was, he kept that to himself. In the meantime, he wanted nothing to do with the chameleon again.

"I got him to repay us for the mugging," Boon said, smirking. But he wouldn't tell when Felix and the others asked. "You'll find out when we get to New York. Now that is a reason to make this crazy plan work."

So once they arrived, Felix got off the bike, adjusted his shirt and headed straight toward the house. Because he was the only one to have been there before, they had agreed he would go in alone, in case Shyuri was not at the garden center in Phuket after all. Their plan, mostly, relied on luck. Tao would wait for him at the mouth of the road near the gate, hoping no one would arrive. As he watched Felix give a final nod and disappear into the greenery, took out a piece of oak and a knife and began to hatch out a praying Buddha statue—praying, no doubt, for them.

With the weather cooler than it had been during his previous visit, the house was more beautiful than ever. Felix paused before approaching the front door, taking in the jasmine, or being taken in by it. There was a stillness about the morning he disliked, although it bode well for his plan. It was very quiet. The tall arches cast a heavy shade over the windows and kept the insides cool and unseen. The grass itself was rich in water and plush—there was a raw humidity to it all. No dry leaves on the ground. The only way Felix realized someone had come up behind him was by feeling a slight give in the earth, as if with too much pressure it would tear a hole and swallow him up.

"What do you want?" The gardener was leaning on a spade as heavy as they made them, and chewing on a spitful of tobacco as he eyed Felix up and down.

Felix gave a short laugh, or rather, all the air rushed out of him. He hadn't considered other people, like the gardener, being here. "I've met you before."

"Is that right?"

"Yes sir," Felix said, giving a wai, "around a week ago."

"I know it, you're the son." Little bits of leaf flew from his mouth as he talked. "Well, Shyuri's not here."

Felix wore an expression he hoped didn't betray his fear. "Could I wait for him?"

The gardener eyed him again. He chewed the tobacco as he considered, but after a while it seemed like he was getting something from between his teeth and had forgotten Felix was standing there, waiting. Just when the boy was about to repeat himself, the gardener spit out the tobacco into the jasmine bush, took out a round tin from his overall's pocket and, with two grimy fingers, worked up a dollop of brown paste he placed newly into his mouth. He looked up at Felix before putting the tin away, considering, but then stowed it deep onto his person again. Suddenly his expression was bored, as if Felix had tried to entertain him in a conversation about something which he didn't care about.

"He's gonna come back around two."

"That's fine. I'll wait."

The gardener frowned as if to say is that right?, but he leaned back from his shovel and moved toward the azalea bushes. "Front door's open." And then, stepping heavily on the grass in the way God might've on the day of its creation, knowing he was the best gardener in all of Phuket, he plodded off to work.

This meetup had cost Felix some time, but he tied his shoe before reaching for the door in an attempt to seem calm and not too eager. Really, it didn't matter. The gardener had already walked off to his next plot of Eden.

Inside the house it was, in fact, cooler. Felix wiped his brow gratefully. After this surprise, he was weary of what else he hadn't planned for. Then again, he scrunched his three point plan up in his pocket and headed toward the study without thinking about it too much.

The second time in the house, he noticed things he hadn't before. The door to the study, for instance, was propped open by two copper goats whose horns curled and pierced the skull right where the eyes would usually be. Felix raised his eyebrows as he moved past. The filing cabinets along the wall were all locked with a key that he assumed was well hidden, and not in plain sight within the desk. Had Boon come with him he'd have spotted the key like a mockingbird does a silver earring in a park. Or, had he brought Tao, he could probably have broken the locks from his years as a locksmith or whatever other similar professions he had dabbled in before ending up on the shore. But Felix had to work with what he was given, so he began to look for a crowbar.

Unlike the rest of the house, which was filled with useless, albeit artistic and oddly shaped objects that, on closer inspection, could've helped him in one way or another, the study was incredibly bare of tools. From an open desk drawer he produced a pencil which he stuck into the lock to no avail. Then, he tried with a paperclip, a safety pin, a letter knife, a binder clip; he stuck in a pen cap—which broke—and then attempted to hack the lock from the side with his driver's license, all the while fiddling with the slide button and swearing when it jammed stuck.

Like any young man whose pride has been hurt, he needed to get his hands on something petty and revengeful. So he took a break to look for the chameleon. He found his way to the library easily where the jewel waited for him in the manner he remembered, green emerald, golden wire, reaching forward with his tiny—

"Gotcha," Felix said, holding it to the light by its tail. He thought about catching a tokay the same way and grinned. Suddenly, he loved Thailand again.

This whole time, however, he had been on edge, and the library, with its stuffy padded walls, quietened all sounds, down to the smallest click of a lighter being opened. His back stiffened. He looked around himself. A clock was set on the opposite side of the room, two granite elephants guarding the hours ticking by as if, like everything else in this house, Shyuri's time was something he didn't want stolen. Well, Felix thought gaily as he stood in the man's house with little security to stop him, well, well, well. Like before, however, his smile dropped as he read the time, and he hurried off to the study with his hands cupped around the small animal, its little feet cold against his palms. He never gave a final glance into the dark room.

Thinking about it on the short way back, he was already frustrated on how he would open the drawers, when an idea came to him. He set the chameleon down on the office desk, then moved back towards the door, grabbed one of the goat statues, and flung it against the closest cabinet. Impossible to crack without a key, but built of thin metal, the drawer popped open like the lid of a mint tin and hit Felix on his pinkie finger. He bit on it but looked back at the chameleon.

"Vive la bonne chance," he muttered, butchering the accent so much he blushed in the empty house before getting to work.

Half an hour later, Felix sat in the middle of the floor with papers in his hand and about half the filing cabinets opened. He had read the document he was holding four times already, and the others on the floor too, but his grip tightened around it. He was focused on the numbers, couldn't look past them actually. With the whole document in Thai, it was odd that the money would be counted in dollars. There were other numbers too, bank accounts and addresses, but this was the one he couldn't move past. The cost and the age.

About three fourths of the cabinets he had opened were full of such papers, stapled in three—a Thai version, one in English, and a third like the one he had stored inside an empty cards box in his drawer since he was five years old, one for the child.

Then, he opened a couple of cabinets full of passports. These were fake, as for every photo there were about ten corresponding names, but they were good copies. Had he not seen them laid alphabetically in a row, he wouldn't have been able to tell. There were young men and women, children, elderly citizens, and even a couple mixed races. Halfway down the 'B' sections he had found Boon's passport, the one that had been stolen in Paris—he smiled at the goatee George had drawn on Boon's face before being approached by the two thugs. Clearly, Shyuri was mixed in that business too—seemed to be the central piece in fact, the coordinator for this type of business.

Suddenly, he couldn't bear to be in the house anymore, not with the sweet jasmine coming in from the open windows or the rustle of leaves from the oleanders. The half-dented drawers, neat with paper, reminded him of school. The goat statues, blind and laying on their sides in real agony. It was not a home, but rather a base from which an ugly root system spread out in all directions and suffocated whatever it could reach.

Holding Boon's passport in one hand and the chameleon in his pocket, Felix was heading toward the front door when he caught sight of the time. It was only midday. He didn't want to meet Shyuri again—that he had established the first time he had been at the house—but he still had some time before the man would return. Felix pondered for a moment, flared his nostrils and he stepped back into the room.

As before, he set the chameleon on the desk watching him, and talked to it like a man would to his brother-in-arms.

"First, the goddamn money," he whispered, and smashed another cabinet open.

As he had gone about his business, he had come to appreciate more and more Shyuri's idea of safety, that is, from the perspective of a thief. Because the business the Big Man conducted was so removed from himself, the house, built in the middle of nowhere, was low on the radar of local criminals. And with the rumor that he never left, and was not much of a host, no one dared to placate their curiosity and visit. It was a house so rarely visited that the only security he needed was the gardener and some lock-and-key cabinets. It was a real pleasure for Felix to find thick stashes of money in the newly opened drawers labeled for the different jobs the Big Man did.

Now, although everything about the situation was messy, Felix wanted to come out clean. He didn't want money that wasn't his. So he quickly shuffled through the list, and miraculously found both of Boon's envelopes, one from Paris and one from the recent exchange of passports in Phuket. Those he grabbed, filling in what A-wut and Decha had spent, but left everything else as was.

Then he approached the middle of the wall, where most of the damage had been done to the cabinets, and took a few moments to pick out a passport with a photo that looked like Tao. He found a couple of options, but settled on one that was just a bit younger and had the same stoic expression of Boon's older brother. He was about done, and had placed his new belongings on the desk when he stopped short again. His plan kept changing, but this time, he smiled a little to himself about it. He returned to the middle cabinet and pulled out two more passports with the same last name as Tao's.

"Do you think they'd want to come?" He asked the chameleon without looking back. And then moved toward the money cabinet. Here his grin faded, but he took an envelope at random, pulled out the money, fanned and counted it, and closed the drawer shut again. He placed the heavy bills in his shirt pocket, rolled tight like a cigar, and his smile returned.

He shrugged at his sparkling companion and said, "For Dara and Yai's flight."

He decided that, already red handed, he might as well have an easier getaway, and for that reason he emptied Shyuri's briefcase, put everything inside, with the chameleon right on top, and stole the briefcase too. At last, he grabbed the pile of papers he had been reading on the floor as well as a stack from the drawers and put them in the bag. *His* bag. He was already savoring the ride back to Dara's house.

With the briefcase bulging with stuff, he was ready to leave, but first he showed himself to the bathroom to clean his hands from all the filthy work he had had to do. The day had been productive, he observed, and it wasn't even two in the afternoon. He hadn't felt so wonderful since the first week in Phuket, when the food still tasted foreign and his accent lagged a breath behind him. Still, he dried his hands quickly. The bathroom, displaying lots of towels embellished with initials, reminded him of something, and it was while he was grabbing the satchel that he saw it, a familiar face. There, perfectly eye-level with the mirror, half-illuminated from the bottom as if it had been done on purpose, was the angel statuette. He felt some sort of longing, a mix of both repulsion and affection. He couldn't resist its ugliness. As he headed out, he swept it clean into his bag.

"Vive le courage too!" he cried into the house, this time without blushing.

Chapter 18

FOR THE FIRST TIME EVER, New York City was quiet. It was a summer day, the first languid day of May, crickets chirping under the flowering cherry blossoms and the cerulean sky bringing out the pink in the tulips and a great drowsiness over the traffic. Felix sat on a bench in Central Park admiring the very tulips that had been pictured in *National Geographic* the previous month. It was the first year New York had ever been featured in an outdoor magazine, and yet no one was talking about it. Indeed, the city was quiet. Well, there were car horns honking down Fifth Avenue, constructions on the south-west corner of the park, and a child crying in his mother's arms because the ducks had flown way across the pond, and *that was too far,* he was trying to say while she shushed him. Felix had not felt so at peace for a long time.

After he and Boon had flown back from Phuket, the weeks passed slowly. Boon had returned to work and Felix to lounging in the presence of his family and everything he had known and grown up to love. He ate donuts for breakfast for a week. He placed his passports, for he had two now, so deep in his desk so he wouldn't have to see them for a couple of months. The angel statuette he arranged next to his bed, and the chameleon near it. Not yet accustomed to the baht, he had taken much more money than he had intended to, and Boon had happily exchanged the jewel for it. Boon had never been the sentimental type.

He knew, however, how to get his way. About a week after they'd arrived, Boon invited Felix over for lunch, an easy affair of sardines and crab curry soup from a recipe that Khun Ao had written on the back of a receipt. Inevitably, the two slipped back in conversation about their trip, at which point Boon extracted a heavy box from a kitchen cabinet, something a grandfather might have stored a lifetime of wax soldiers in. It was wonderfully embellished with gold paint, the aluminum thick, yellow and expensive. Boon set it on the table and gracefully pulled off the lid, uncovering rows of honey-brown half-spheres in fluted paper cups.

"*Marron Glacés*," Boon said, picking one up and putting it in his mouth. "I had Cousin George send them over. He's a prig and he is punctual, a punctual prig and a prig about being punctual. Still, these arrived yesterday just as we agreed." And to Boon's own credit, not a single paper cup was missing.

As part of his compensation, Boon had also arranged for George to send Shyuri's documents to the Thai authorities. With his position in the French bank and Vivi's power in such matters—come to think of it, something that Felix still didn't know much about—Phuket's justice department had acted quickly, much more than if the lead had come from two boys in flip flops.

Really, there was no reason for Felix and Boon to stress out about being followed. New York was as full of crime as any city. Yet, as the eldest, Boon drank all day and Felix washed it down with more coffee than what Boon drank to begin with. They called each other frequently, just a couple of blocks away, speaking in quick little breaths of fear, saying little, before returning to their nervous ways.

Luckily, the child trafficking agency was overturned, as said the headline in a newspaper George had sent over. There had been some investigations and some well-chosen informants that led the police straight to the Big Man, but of course Felix only knew the little they covered in the story. The Big Man had had no time to get away. He had asked some of the most senior members to help him tie up the business and leave, but many crooks run when they smell trouble. Decha had been one of the few caught alongside the Big Man, but there was no news of A-wut. In such a position, a man could have gathered his family and possessions, bought night bus tickets into Bangkok and disappeared into its labyrinth of streets. In the city, maybe, he could set up a tool shop, a *bazaar*, selling everything from spoons to lightbulbs to the most effective lock-picking sets, making a few if only quiet friends. He could change his name, make new identities if needed. Then again, no one knew what became of him after he disappeared.

All this was not addressed by the newspaper. There were only a couple of names and figures and not much about it at all. It was something the police wanted to keep quiet, to ease panic. And so was a sketchy ending to many sketchy lives of crime.

Sitting on the bench with his hands on his knees, the rafflesia business behind him, Felix had one day at peace. The next day would be the gloomiest Memorial Day to date, the sky upset with the impurities of the world, heavy with rain in the hopes of cleansing itself. Boon would pick Felix up at seven thirty, a week unshaved, they would skip dinner and head straight to the airport. But for the moment, Felix closed his eyes against the sun and took a breath of petunias and pansies and all else sprouting along the paths of the park. On the other side of the lake, the ducks clamored at another child, hungry for bread.

The car made JFK to Newark, thirty-three miles through the city, in under forty minutes—it was the fastest time a vehicle had ever moved through New York. Contrary to belief, with so little alcohol in the bottle chocolates and so much sugar, Boon's reaction times had, in fact, improved. Distracted by executing the best getaway, he had forgotten to feel sick.

"C'mon," Felix urged him forward, holding his breath at each turn.

He had lowered the window in order to see better, and was sprayed with water running off the windshield. There was no time to spare, they soldiered on. Occasionally Boon would hear Felix chant *c'mon, c'mon*, so that with his Knicks hat, he truly did look like a fan.

Like JFK, Newark was short of organized. There were cars parked everywhere, spilling onto the sidewalk to make space for other cars to park next to them on the curb. Here, however, people seemed too concerned with the rain and getting in and out quickly to issue problems with it. It was an airport, it was messy, and everyone closed an eye. It was that type of day too.

Boon couldn't find an open spot along the front, so he pulled into a parking garage and pretty quickly they were out of the car, running toward the stairs shaft that led to the arrivals hall. Felix thought he was a lighting flash just as the door closed behind them.

They took the steps two by two and then, in fours. Each turn they sped up. When they fell through the *Arrivals* door into the airport, they had no breath left to talk. Boon took out their napkin, the writing miraculously intact, and pointed toward the right. Again they took off, slower this time. Felix was well aware of his state: dark clothes drenched with water, stained with chocolate, his eyes bulging and dark, reeking, most likely, of New York's sewers and muddy water. Boon reeked even more, having fallen into a puddle earlier in the evening. At least, people thought as the two boys swept through the pristine halls under surgical white lights, they were just Knicks fans and not two goddamn tourists.

The two remained silent as they continued their quest at the correct arrivals gate, but there were people from another flight making their exit now. No Thai faces to be seen.

Felix caught Boon's eye, his forehead creased. "What if they didn't pass?"

"If customs stopped them? If they realized the passports were fake?"

Felix nodded. "Would they be sent to prison? Sent back?"

Boon shrugged and shook his head—he didn't know what to think. He ran a hand over his beard and sighed. "Let's just keep looking," he said, tugging Felix's sleeve toward the commercial wing of the airport. "We are late after all. Let's just keep going."

Newark airport, like modern designs of many things that try to make something ugly *interesting* instead, was shaped to look like a green bean, meaning that from one position it was impossible to see the rest of the airport. Not long after taking off again, they found themselves in a hall lined in food stalls and tourist shops. Completely different people. Many of them.

Something that Felix loved about Boon, was his beady eyes. Just as he was about to suggest they leave, looking up at the ceiling trying to figure out if it was still raining and how he would be able to sleep that night, Boon pointed to a scarf shop on the opposite side of the room. As they advanced, they could see a family huddled around some racks of sports scarves, trying to look interested in them. From their expression it was obviously a strain.

But Felix had broken into a smile. "I wonder if the Knicks won," he said under his breath, and Boon struggled to keep himself from running up to them.

Just then, Dara turned and saw them approaching. She nudged Tao and Yai and the three stood smiling, stupefied by the uncertainty of having really made it. They had had no problems at customs—and why would they? With American passports, traveling together, they really *had* looked like a family.

Neither side hurried now, they were savoring the moment.

Boon turned to Felix then, and cracked a grin he couldn't hold back. "What should we show them first? Where should we go?"

Felix beamed back, "I know a place."

"Mr Wanchai's?"

"Well I'd like to," Felix replied, forgetting that he was cold and it was late, "but he's too busy."

"Isn't he always?" Boon said, scratching his sideburns.

"Yeah, but you know how the holidays hit him the most. It is Memorial day after all."

The two kept walking forward, the family radiant in front of so many colorful scarves and pom poms and thousands of imaginary cheers. The airport drummed with activity, the wheels of suitcases on the shiny floor, a barista making a coffee at three in the morning.

"How goddamn unfortunate," Boon said, but he was smiling.

ACKNOWLEDGEMENTS

FIRSTLY, I WANT TO FORMALLY thank my Creative Writing teachers at Charleston County School of the Arts, F. Rutledge Hammes, Beth Webb Hart and Danielle Detiberus, who spent the last three years shaping me into the writer I am today. Thank you for taking a chance on the kid coming from abroad who called the hallways *corridors*, and still does sometimes. Evidently, there is still work to be done.

I would like to thank John Thompson, author of three award winning novels, who has served as my mentor through the process of writing this book and had read all that I have written, giving plenty of edits, even when time fell short. This book would not be what it is without your help.

Mostly, however, I would like to thank my father, for reading, and re-reading, and re-re-reading every single page that did or didn't make it in this book. He has spent more hours than I could admit on this book—he knows the book inside and out and beyond that too. From the development of the plot, to fleshing out the story, to fixing odd commas and debating the use of a word, you've been by my side through the thick of it all. As in my dedication, I couldn't ask for a better audience. There aren't enough words—*quindi, grazie e grazie mille Pino.*

As Aesop says in "The Lion and the Mouse," *Little friends may prove to be big friends.* Well, I'd like to thank all my friends and peers—namely Merrik Moriarty for her unmatched imagination; my darling Cooper, for endless, *honest*, conversations; Jessie Leitzel, for our struggle to juggle everything together—and too many more.

Thank you to my family for showing me the world and inspiring my love of cultures. Thank you to my mother, who has supported me, always. To my cover artist, Maggie Largent: thank you for patiently hearing my crazy ideas and for bringing them to life.

Finally, I have a special thanks for a friend, currently about 3,490 miles and an ocean apart, without whom my account of Thailand would have fallen completely short of reality. Panpan, let's use this book as an excuse to meet again, in Thailand, hopefully, where you can show me that there *aren't* any buses in Phuket after all. I miss you, let's get hot chocolate soon.

ABOUT THE AUTHOR

Born in Milan, Italy, Linda Garziera grew up among classic Lombard landscapes— wheat-heavy countrysides and industrial centers just an hour from the Swiss border. With her spontaneous family, or because of it, she has lived most of her life on the road, so by third grade, when her family relocated to England, she had already developed a palate for cultures. Linda would spend the next seven years learning the language and exploring strictly British landscapes. Primarily, she attributes her love for reading and writing to this time, the authors Roald Dahl, Jaqueline Wilson and David Walliams, and the wonderful hills and parks of Shrewsbury, Shropshire. When she moved to South Carolina, USA, she continued exploring this passion for language by joining the Creative Writing program at Charleston County School of the Arts. Her experiences living in three countries have and will continue to serve as settings for her best fiction. So far, her writing has gained recognition in Scholastic Writing Awards, the Atlantic Institute, and the 2023 Kelly Writers House Anthology by the University of Pennsylvania Press, and she is a contribution editor on the literary magazine *Trace Fossils Review*. Fueled by her fiery curiosity, Linda Garziera will continue writing at Duke University, where she will be studying Economics. As Zooey Glass (from *Franny and Zooey*, JD Salinger) once said, "Beauty is my Achilles' heel." Well, for Linda, it is capturing the feeling of a place and recreating it on a page. It is with this wish that she writes.

Made in the USA
Middletown, DE
02 August 2024